Frederick Law Olmsted's

Point Chautauqua

THE STORY OF AN HISTORIC LAKESIDE COMMUNITY

Author ❧ EDGAR C. CONKLING

Photo Editor ❧ JOYCE MORRIS

Canisius College Press

First published in the United States of
America in 2001 by Canisius College Press.

Copyright pending.

For more information, contact:
Canisius College Press
2001 Main Street
Buffalo, NY 14208

Publisher: Joseph F. Bieron

Library of Congress
Catalog Card number: 2001 135056

Layout Design: Anne-Marie Dobies
Photo Editor: Joyce Morris

ISBN 0-9671480-6-5
Printed in United States of America

TO RENAN
(1955 – 2000)

TABLE OF CONTENTS

LIST OF ILLUSTRATIONS

I

This book is sponsored by
The Point Chautauqua Historical Preservation Society
in compliance with the provisions of its
Charter with The State University of New York.

PAST AND PRESENT MEMBERS OF THE SOCIETY

State of the Arts

NYSCA

This book is made possible with public funds from
The New York State Council on the Arts, a state agency.

Additional funding has been provided by
Robert and Ertem Beckman.

FOREWORD

$\mathscr{I}$t has been my good fortune to know Ed and Helen Conkling for many years. It was Frederick Law Olmsted who brought us together. As an architectural historian interested in Olmsted and his circle, I recall meeting the Conklings and their friend Ertem Beckman in the early 1980s on a bus tour of Olmsted's Buffalo park system. At the time, we had the first of many conversations about the religious resort community that Olmsted had laid out in 1875 at Point Chautauqua and that was their year-round home.

Olmsted's plan for Point Chautauqua distinguishes it from other summer communities that were developed in Upstate New York in the nineteenth century. It poses a striking contrast to the Chautauqua Institution, located across the lake. Indeed, we have every reason to believe that Olmsted intended Point Chautauqua to be an instructive comparison to its more famous neighbor. Olmsted had condemned the Institution's prosaic grid pattern of streets because it denied residents a sense of connection with the lovely lakeside site. He also found the crowding together of buildings at the Institution unhealthy. Taking a very different approach, Olmsted laid out Point Chautauqua on a far more spacious and imaginative plan. Its curving streets follow the sloping landscape and allow lot owners to enjoy views of the lake and refreshing breezes from the water. Like his earlier projects for Riverside near Chicago, Parkside in Buffalo, and Tacoma, Washington, Point Chautauqua anticipated the layout of many twentieth-century suburban residential communities.

Together with Ertem Beckman, Ed and Helen Conkling have been the driving force behind the movement to celebrate and preserve Point Chautauqua's significant heritage. They were the first to undertake the research that unearthed much of the information contained in this book. Armed with knowledge, they mobilized their friends and neighbors to take steps to preserve their historic community. Largely because of their efforts, and the able professional assistance of Barbara Campagna, Point Chautauqua was listed on the National Register of Historic Places in 1996. It was a long and sometimes frustrating struggle; one can only admire their perseverance in face of many delays and detours that were thrown in their path. One of their most trying tasks was to convince the staff of the New York Office of Parks, Recreation and Historic Preservation that the streets – which for the most part conform to Olmsted's plan – were significant in and of themselves, and despite the loss of the public spaces Olmsted had mapped out. As a result of their efforts, New York State and the nation have become aware of one of the forgotten masterpieces of America's greatest landscape architect.

I cherish fond memories of visits to the Conklings at Point Chautauqua. One in particular I remember, perhaps the earliest, was made with Charles Beveridge, the leading Olmsted scholar. After a splendid lunch at the Conklings' home, our hosts, equipped with a copy of Olmsted's plan, took us on a walking tour of Point Chautauqua's quiet streets. That afternoon I discovered one of the truly special places of Western New York. This book will ensure that present and future generations will know the meaning of Point Chautauqua. And I expect that readers will also glean from its pages an appreciation of the author's steadfast attachment to this noteworthy community and his unselfish devotion to its continued well-being. ❧

FRANCIS R. KOWSKY
Buffalo, NY ❧ March 2001

PREFACE

*T*his book is about a work of art, one whose value derives not only from its beauty and rarity but, more particularly, from the eminence of the artist. As a well-preserved creation of America's most celebrated landscape architect, Point Chautauqua's 1875 Frederick Law Olmsted design has been listed on the National Register of Historic Places.

Among Olmsted's many works, Point Chautauqua stands alone. Only here did the master find a physical setting that conformed to his aesthetic ideal – a wooded hillside rising steeply from the shores of a lovely body of water. Moreover, this was his only design for a religious community. Despite these unique features, however, Point Chautauqua richly exhibits the design principles that are the hallmarks of every Olmsted creation. This community therefore offers a rewarding laboratory for students of historic landscape architecture.

The passage of a century and a quarter since Olmsted laid out this community has supplied it with additional layers of historic accumulation. Since its beginnings Point Chautauqua has experienced a series of changes in character and function, from Bible camp to hotel resort to lakeside residential community. Each phase in this evolution left its mark, most noticeably in the representative house types that have survived. Thus the Point Chautauqua of today remains a storehouse of cultural history.

Yet, despite its obvious worth for all who appreciate its special historical significance, Point Chautauqua's Olmsted design is fragile. For not only is this a priceless artifact of history, it is also a living, working community of people with a wide variety of life experiences, values, and interests. On occasion those interests may appear at variance with the need to protect Olmsted's handiwork. It is an irony that the beautiful natural setting ingeniously shaped by

Olmsted tends to attract economic forces that would threaten its very existence.

The greatest threat arises from the potential actions of property owners, community leaders, and political officials who may be ill-informed as to the nature and value of their heritage. In a lakeside community, where some property owners are in residence only during the short summer season, such knowledge may sometimes be lacking. Sadly, the history of Point Chautauqua records a number of occasions when uninformed actions by members of the community have led to the loss of significant pieces of the Olmsted legacy.

My first – and most compelling – reason for writing this book, therefore, is to help residents of Olmsted's Point Chautauqua and other decision-makers to gain an appreciation for the rare national treasure with which they have been entrusted. It is my aim to make them aware of their responsibility to preserve the integrity of the Olmsted design, not only for the benefit of their own descendants, but for all Americans, to whom it also belongs. I hope to show, too, that the preservation of a work by Olmsted is not limited to maintaining the general configuration of the design. In a fuller measure, it also requires a sensitivity to the essential spirit of that design, in particular Olmsted's abiding devotion to the ideal of naturalness.

It is my belief, too, that the story of Point Chautauqua is relevant to the many other Olmsted creations throughout the United States and Canada. Essentially all of his works share the Olmsted principles embodied in the Point Chautauqua design; consequently, they are susceptible to the same preservation problems that these attractive qualities seem to engender. As those in the broader community who are devoted to the work of Olmsted become informed of the stresses to which this Olmsted design is subject, they will no doubt find them very similar to the perils with which they must cope in their own locales. The cooperation that prevails among such interest groups and the defenses they share depend upon such exchanges of information as this.

Many people have helped with this book as it evolved during a decade of community efforts to safeguard the Olmsted design. From the outset, this writing has drawn importantly upon the diligent library research undertaken by Ertem Beckman and my wife, Helen Conkling, both past presidents of the Point Chautauqua Historical Preservation Society. Helen also designed the walking tour [Appendix], which reveals so well her love of natural beauty, and especially the scenic vistas at Point Chautauqua, and the wildflowers and blooming plants that abound in its woods and meadows. She, too, has been my severest and most helpful critic throughout the writing process.

And, of course, none of this would have been possible without the devoted and enthusiastic efforts of the members of the Historical Preservation Society during the past several years. They, in turn, drew inspiration from the pioneering efforts of those dedicated individuals who rediscovered this Olmsted treasure and brought it to our attention: Claire Ross, Joan Bozer, and Pricilla Nixon. Two others who provided invaluable service to us in our efforts to save Point Chautauqua were Tania Werbizky of the Preservation League, whose wise counsel has helped us at critical moments, and consultant Barbara Campagna, whose skill and experience were so vital in securing our National Register listing. Essential moral and material support for the work of the Society – and the Historical Committee that preceded it – came, too, from the officers and members of the Point Chautauqua Association, as well as officials of the Town of Chautauqua.

The illustrations are an integral part of this book. For these I am indebted to a number of persons, most of all Joyce Morris, who has very capably filled the role of photo editor. Over a period of months Joyce has searched local museums and collections to put together a number of rare historic photographs that portray Point Chautauqua in its different epochs in a way that no living person could otherwise imagine. She has also worked closely with laboratory technicians to ensure that these old images are seen at their best. I am very grateful to the donors of these illustrative materials: Ertem Beckman, Helen Campbell, Jerry and Gladys Loth, the Fenton and McClurg Museums, Jane

Currie, Joan Hicks, John Sirianno, Diana Holt, Jane Nelson, and the National Park Service Olmsted Historic Site at Brookline, Massachusetts.

Special thanks are due the Department of Geography at the State University of New York at Buffalo and its chairman, Hugh Calkins, who supplied the facilities and financial support for preparation of the computer-drawn maps used in this book. I am very indebted to cartographer Emil Boasson, who undertook this work with such exceptional skill and taste.

Finally, I want to express my deep appreciation to Professor Francis R. Kowsky, who has done so much for the preservation of Point Chautauqua and has helped in a great many other ways. It was Frank's eloquent tribute to the historical significance and integrity of Olmsted's Point Chautauqua design that convinced the New York State Board of Historic Preservation of the need to extend official recognition of its importance. On a number of occasions since, Frank has been quick to come to the defense of the Olmsted design and to give substantial support for the work of the Historical Preservation Society. His encouragement and valuable suggestions have contributed immeasurably to the writing of this book. ❧

EDGAR C. CONKLING

An Incomparable Place

THE OLMSTED BRAND

"*T*he moment I saw Point Chautauqua, I knew that it was
an Olmsted design," remarked a visitor to this Victorian-era

community on the north-
eastern shore of Lake
Chautauqua. William
Parment, an architect be-
fore his election to the New
York State Assembly, had
recognized at once the
winding roads, the widely
spaced dwellings, the
scenic views, and the rustic
natural charm of this
community's wooded slopes
as hallmarks of that preemi-
nent nineteenth-century
pioneer of American
landscape architecture,
Frederick Law Olmsted
[Figure 1]. Olmsted schol-

Figure 1 ❧ Olmsted roadways. The visitor's first impression of Point
Chautauqua is of tree-lined roads winding gently downward toward the
lakeshore. Curving roads that follow the contour of the land are a
hallmark of the eminent nineteenth-century landscape architect Frederick
Law Olmsted, who designed this community in 1875. Shown here in a
contemporary sketch are the intersections of three residential streets: In
the foreground, Midland Avenue descends from the left to meet Floral
Avenue, rising from below. Beyond is the northern entrance to Lake
Avenue, which parallels the lakeshore, separated from the water by a
half-mile-long strip of land called The Strand. The triangular wooded
area on the far right is a remnant of Olmsted's Elm Park.
❧ From a sketch by Jane Nelson

ars agree that Point Chautauqua holds a special place among
the master's works. In his long career Olmsted planned only a
handful of residential communities; among these, Point
Chautauqua is the only one intended expressly as a religious

retreat. In 1996 the United States Department of the Interior placed Point Chautauqua on the National Register of Historic Places in recognition of its well-preserved Olmsted design.

No residential community created by Frederick Law Olmsted better expresses the philosophy and design principles of that master than Point Chautauqua. Drawing upon a life of service to humanity and endowed with a deep appreciation for natural beauty, Olmsted conceived of Point Chautauqua as a wholesome forest refuge away from the pressures of the city. He therefore drew his plan for this settlement in such a way as to bring its people together into a close-knit community. The spirit of togetherness and belonging found in today's Point Chautauqua is testimony to Olmsted's success in realizing his objectives. It was a happy circumstance, too, that here the master found the ideal physical setting for achieving these goals.

Point Chautauqua does indeed have a different feel from the many other residential communities ringing the 58-mile shoreline of Lake Chautauqua. This unique character traces directly to its Olmsted origins. It is especially apparent from the way in which the master accommodated his plan to the distinctive physical environment of the Lake Chautauqua district, a forested, hilly terrain overlooking a great expanse of water. Today Point Chautauqua is a community of ninety-some families situated on a hillside rising from a prominent point of land that emerges from the northern basin of the lake. Neighboring lake communities, on similarly sloping land, have been laid out in the conventional gridiron pattern and, as a result, their streets descend abruptly to the shore. By contrast, the Olmsted-designed avenues of Point Chautauqua follow the contour of the land as they wind gently downward, offering at every turn tempting vistas of the serenely blue waters of Lake Chautauqua.

LAKE CHAUTAUQUA AND ITS REGION

*T*his exquisite body of water lies within a narrow, winding valley in the forested Allegheny foothill country of southwestern New York State [Figure 2]. The hills rising *en echelon* above the lake on either side display the rounded forms typical of this glaciated sector of the Appalachian Plateau. Adding further to the captivating beauty of this natural setting is the distant view in the east of the rugged unglaciated peaks of the high Alleghenies, which are visible when atmospheric conditions are right [Thompson 1970, pp. 19-23, 33]. At the end of a warm summer day, Point Chautauqua affords a splendid view of the sun setting in the west behind the crest of a ridge top reaching 1,565 feet above sea level. Beyond this escarpment lies a steep 1,022-foot descent to the Lake Erie shore a dozen miles farther west.

At an elevation of 1,308 feet above sea level, Lake Chautauqua is one of the highest large bodies of freshwater in the country. It differs from the geologically similar Finger Lakes of Central New York in that Chautauqua's waters drain into the Allegheny River and thence southward into the Ohio-Mississippi system, whereas the Finger Lakes flow into the Great Lakes-St. Lawrence system [Thompson 1970, p. 33]. The ridge top that separates Chautauqua Valley from the Lake Erie Basin is therefore a continental divide, an accident of geology that helped shape the history of the entire region. Taking advantage of this situation, the French forces during their war with the British were able to make a short portage from Lake Erie, up over the escarpment and down into Lake Chautauqua. From there they sailed their canoes down the Allegheny River to supply their outpost at Fort Duquesne (later to become Pittsburgh). In taking this route, the French were following a path that had been used by the Indians from the earliest times.

When the Revolutionary War freed Western New York from British and Indian control, this "Portage Trail" became an avenue for a wave of American settlers. The dense forests of elm, red maple, oak, and northern hardwoods constituted one of the earliest attractions, forming the basis for the furniture

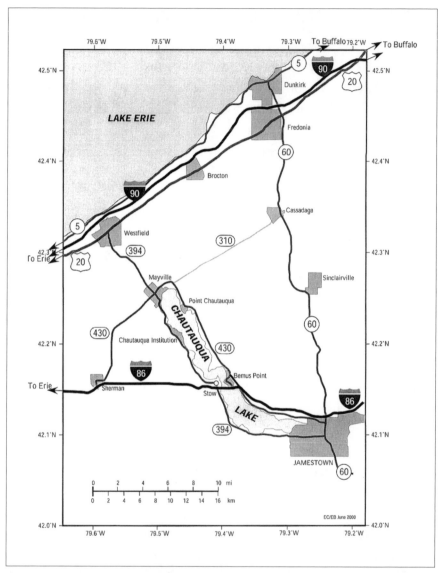

Figure 2 ❧ The Chautauqua region. Point Chautauqua is one of many resort communities ringing the 58-mile shoreline of Lake Chautauqua. The lake rests within a narrow, glacially carved valley in the Allegheny foothills of western New York. The wooded hills rising above the lake lie at the northern limit of the great Appalachian Plateau, which ends in a steep 1,022-foot drop to the shore of Lake Erie. With its great scenic beauty and magnificent lakes, the Chautauqua region is a prime vacation land serving the tri-state area of western New York, northwestern Pennsylvania, and northeastern Ohio.

❧ Map by Emil Boasson, Computer Cartography Laboratory, Department of Geography, SUNY/Buffalo

and woodworking industries that soon sprang up at the southern end of Lake Chautauqua and centered upon Jamestown [Thompson 1970, Chap. 2]. Other rural service centers arose along the route of the Portage Trail, at Barcelona Harbor, Westfield, Mayville, and Bemus Point. Other than lumbering and manufacturing wood products, the main activity in the Allegheny hill country at the time was a poor type of mixed farming, hampered by the thin, unproductive shale-based soils and by distance from urban markets. The region had not yet become incorporated into the North American Dairy Belt. Original title to the area was held by the Holland Land Company, from which the new settlers purchased their property. Among these were the Leet family, from whom the initial Point Chautauqua Association obtained 106 acres of land in 1875.

This was the setting for the Bible camp laid out in 1875 by Frederick Law Olmsted for a group from the American Baptist Church. Today the site is little changed in area and general configuration from that appearing on the original Olmsted map of November 1, 1875.[1] A century and a quarter later, Olmsted's characteristically curving roads and pathways and his layout and numbering of the lots remain virtually intact. The roads still bear the names he gave them.

The community is bounded by a golf course on its northwest side, the lake on the west and southeast, and a cluster of houses called Tinkertown Bay on the east. Located at the northeastern end of Lake Chautauqua, three miles from Mayville, it is almost directly across the lake from the grounds of Chautauqua Institution. New York State Route 430 runs north of Point Chautauqua, and it is from this highway that one enters Leet Avenue, which leads into the Point. Forming an irregular crescent, Leet reaches Route 430 at two places and thus provides both an upper and a lower entrance [Figure 3]. From this semicircular drive, other tributary roadways branch off into the community grounds. With this imaginative design feature, Olmsted was able not

---

[1] The area occupied by contemporary Point Chautauqua is identical to that described as the Point Chautauqua Residential District in the Town of Chautauqua Zoning Law (Local Law No. 2-1977), Section 1-04, Subsection 2, Paragraph a, with the addition of lots 246-253 as they appear on the map entitled "Point Chautauqua Grounds," laid out by Professor Frederick Law Olmsted, dated November 1, 1875, filed in the Chautauqua County Clerk's Office in Cabinet 1, Section A, Map 95.

Figure 3 ✺ The middle section of Leet Avenue. The sinuous character of Olmsted's roadways becomes apparent the moment one enters the community, as this contemporary sketch demonstrates. The wooded area on the right is the site once occupied by the Tabernacle, the central meeting place in early Bible-camp days. Leet Avenue broadly assumes the form of a crescent that connects the northern and southern entrances. Branching off this middle section of Leet are other roads that lead into the heart of the community. By this characteristic Olmsted device, Leet effectively serves as a shelter from the outside world. ✺ Sketch by Jane Nelson

only to insulate Point Chautauqua from the hurried outside world but also to offer a sheltered, tree-lined avenue that anticipates the tranquil atmosphere of the community beyond.

The man who created this enduring plan for Point Chautauqua is widely regarded as the most eminent landscape architect of the nineteenth century. Frederick Law Olmsted's genius was his remarkable ability to employ a material artifact – a roadway or park system – to achieve societal goals. He skillfully positioned public lands in the most effective locations for inspiring social interaction, and configured the roadways in such a way as to lead community members to these places of assembly. To appreciate Olmsted's success in attaining these goals at Point Chautauqua, we need to trace the origins of his ideals and see how these shaped the principles that guided his work.

C H A P T E R ❧ T W O

Point Chautauqua's Creator

*T*he abundant accounts of Olmsted's life and work offer a clear record of the many influences that came together in his thinking and supplied the conceptual foundation that enabled him to become a leading founder of American landscape architecture. It is possible to trace his professional lineage to that small group of gardeners and planners who preceded him in Europe and America, to the New England intellectual climate within which he was immersed, and to the life experiences of his remarkably varied career [Figure 4].

Figure 4 ❧ Frederick Law Olmsted as a young man. Son of a prosperous New England merchant family, Olmsted came to his ultimate professional calling by way of a remarkable series of seminal experiences. Growing up in the lovely Connecticut Valley and instilled with a great love of natural beauty from an early age by his parents, he traveled extensively in England and Continental Europe, visiting the newly established public parks of that era. During the course of the tour he reported on his adventures to an American newspaper, and later he pursued a journalistic career that brought him into close contact with the foremost social thinkers of the time. This led eventually to his first landscaping commission, which, in partnership with Calvert Vaux, produced the "Greensward" design for New York's Central Park.

❧ Photo courtesy of the National Park Service, Frederick Law Olmsted National Historic Site

7
❧

OLMSTED'S PROFESSIONAL ORIGINS

English Influences

One of the seminal experiences of Olmsted's youth – long before he was to discover his ultimate lifework – was a trip that he and his brother John made to England. On a walking tour of that country, he visited large new public parks, notably the one at Birkenhead, across the River Mersey from Liverpool. A rural park by the great designer Joseph Paxton intended for the enjoyment of "citizens of every class," Birkenhead Park impressed him deeply [Chadwick 1966, p. 71], inspiring a series of letters home, which were published in the *Hartford Courant*. The parks of London affected him similarly. Later he was to remark that "nothing interested me in London like the parks, and yet I thought a great deal more might be made of them" [Roper 1973, p. 124]. He also visited parks in France, Germany, and Italy and was able to contrast the symmetrical, formally arranged landscapes traditional in those countries with the more natural landscaping that had evolved in England during the eighteenth century.[2] Also beginning to appear on the continent at the time were newer park designs that foretold the spreading influence of the English natural look.

One of the English originators of this natural type of design was Lancelot Brown (better known as "Capability" Brown), who employed a curving pathway in the estates he designed – a path that led through trees to views. Brown believed that all designs should imitate nature: that is, they should have curved forms. "Needless to say, the roads in a Brown park are never straight; they always follow a gentle flowing route" [Turner 1985, p. 79]. Brown surrounded his parks with trees. Carrying this idea of naturalness still further, Humphry Repton developed the concept of *The Picturesque*. He felt that the roughness and irregularity that occur naturally in the landscape should be maintained, and that those rough features should not be smoothed out but made use of. In other words, the design should be adapted to the land, not the other way around. The parks of Brown and Repton were actually deer parks created for the nobil-

8

---

[2] See Frederick Law Olmsted, *Walks and Talks of an American Farmer in England*. London: David Bogue, 1852a.

ity and landed gentry. In time, English social thinkers succeeded in promoting the notion that ordinary citizens deserved equivalents of these "gentlemen's parks." The outcome of this movement was the great English "public" park that so excited Olmsted's interest [Newton 1971, p. 220].

The individual who brought these ideas to the United States was Andrew Jackson Downing, who was busily introducing them here at the time of his unfortunate death by drowning at the age of 38. The first major landscape designer in this country, Downing was also editor of *The Horticulturist*. It was he who began the campaign to create Central Park. Olmsted visited him in 1851 at Newburgh. Downing helped Olmsted formulate his ideas and in general became an important mentor for him.

Intellectual Milieu

During Olmsted's lifetime the United States was deeply preoccupied with antislavery reform and the Civil War, then Reconstruction and the failure of Reconstruction, and later the flood of immigrants. Severe crowding and poverty in the cities bred social problems of all kinds. As a young journalist on assignment in the South, Olmsted saw bad roads, shabby living conditions, inadequate schools and churches, and little evidence of civilization as he perceived it [Olmsted 1856b]. In 1857 no city in the United States had a large public park, no place where city dwellers could get away from crowded tenements. The impact of his encounters with these social problems stayed with Olmsted all his life and doubtless contributed to the dedication that was evidenced in his work as a planner.

As a journalist, the young Olmsted also became acquainted with powerful reformers of the day, heroic persons striving to improve social and economic conditions. Through association with these individuals, and from what he had seen for himself, he formed his ideals for communities – ideals that guided his work ever after.

Early Life Experiences

Olmsted acquired his great love for natural beauty from his parents, who, being prosperous, could afford to take the family on long trips, looking for scenic places throughout the Northeast and in Canada. Frederick Law was deeply influenced by his father, who, he said later, taught him "the most important thing" in his life. He told of this in his biographical writings:

> On a Sunday evening we were crossing the meadows alone. I was tired and he had taken me in his arms. I soon noticed that he was inattentive to my prattle and looking in his face saw in it something unusual. Following the direction of his eyes, I said: "Oh! there's a star." Then he said something of Infinite Love with a tone and manner which really moved me, chick that I was, so much that it has ever since remained in my heart.[3]

Olmsted took a long time finding his chosen career. Before doing so, he was occupied for a time as a farmer, first in Connecticut and later on Staten Island. Farming provided him with a knowledge of soils, and it also gave him experience in organizing work and directing large groups of laborers. He soon wearied of farming, however, and travel drew him. On one such adventure he spent two years as an ordinary seaman on the sailing ship *Ronaldson*, which navigated around the Cape of Good Hope to China [Roper 1973].

A second foreign adventure, the 1850 walking tour of England described above, inspired another of his early enthusiasms. Publication of the letters describing these experiences led him to take up a career in journalism and writing. Prior to the Civil War, he spent several years traveling in the South to report to Northern readers of the *Times* on the economic aspects of slavery. Subsequently he published two books on these subjects and became managing editor of a new literary magazine with responsibility for dealing with contribu-

---

[3] Frederick Law Olmsted, Jr., and Theodora Kimball, eds., *Frederick Law Olmsted, Landscape Architect, 1822-1903* (New York: G. P. Putnam's Sons, 1970), as quoted in Stephenson 1977, p. 5.

tors. This phase of his career led to induction into the select circle of journalists and opinion-makers of the period, providing professional connections that were to prove valuable to his subsequent planning ventures [Rybczynski 1999].

Olmsted and Vaux

It was almost by accident that Olmsted stumbled upon his true calling. In 1857 the British-born architect Calvert Vaux persuaded Olmsted to join him in submitting a plan to a competition for a new Central Park in New York City. Vaux and Olmsted thereupon formed what proved to be an unusually productive collaboration, each bringing to the work a unique set of skills [Kowsky 1998, Chap. 6]. Aided by endorsements from Olmsted's many "literary connections," especially Washington Irving, the partners were declared in the spring of 1858 to have the winning design. The backing of influential sponsors aside, the Olmsted-Vaux plan, "Greensward," received widespread acclaim at the time, and it is still judged superior to the 32 other designs with which it competed [Rybczynski 1999, pp. 163-64]. The many innovative ideas introduced by Olmsted and Vaux into their Central Park plan continue to influence landscape design everywhere [Figure 5].

11

Figure 5 ⸙ The Olmsted-Vaux "Greensward" plan for Central Park. Olmsted's career as a landscape architect began in 1858, when he and English-born architect Calvert Vaux submitted the winning design for New York City's new Central Park. Thus began a fruitful collaboration between two remarkably creative intellects, each of whom contributed a distinct set of valuable skills to the partnership.
ⸯ Courtesy of the National Park Service, Frederick Law Olmsted National Historic Site

The board appointed Olmsted architect-in-chief to oversee construction of the park and named Vaux his assistant. Having thus finally settled upon his lifework, Olmsted at last found all of his seemingly unrelated past experiences coming together. The love of nature inherited from his parents, the knowledge of soil materials and management skills gained from his farming years, the great variety of landscapes and ways of living witnessed in his travels – all of these helped equip him for the new challenge. And now, drawing upon Vaux's knowledge and experience, he knew exactly what to do and flung himself into the work with enthusiasm and intensity. Thereafter Olmsted and Vaux worked together on many other important design projects.

In the meantime, however, the Civil War intruded to send Olmsted in a wholly different direction, but one that would once again add valuable new skills and experiences. He accepted the position of resident secretary (chief executive officer) of the United States Sanitary Commission. This was a civilian agency authorized by President Lincoln to check on health and sanitation conditions among the troops, to advise the army Medical Bureau, and later to organize medical supplies and transportation for the wounded. (Ultimately this organization evolved into the Red Cross.) The end of the war found Olmsted managing the Mariposa gold mines in California, an ill-conceived venture he pursued in an effort to restore his flagging finances. Some good came of it, however: during extensive travels throughout California he came to appreciate the importance of preserving the country's natural wonders, notably Yosemite, and he joined in a successful drive to create a national park system.

While in California Olmsted also received a number of commissions for landscape designs on the West Coast, notably the campus for the future University of California at Berkeley. Throughout this period he continued to develop further his philosophy for landscape architecture, its integral part in the physical arrangement of a community, and the contribution it should make to people's health and mental and social well-being. To Olmsted, parks laid out along natural lines and with beautiful vistas produced a "civilizing influence."

Subsequently, at the urging of Calvert Vaux, he returned to New York to renew their partnership. Together they resumed supervising the development of Central Park and the creation of Brooklyn's magnificent Prospect Park.

The firm of Olmsted, Vaux & Co. continued to prosper as more and more commissions came their way. Among their many achievements were the zoological gardens near Central Park, renovation of Brooklyn's Washington Park, a new campus for Cornell University, a college campus in Maine, an elaborate system of parks for Buffalo, the community of Riverside, Illinois, and South Park in Chicago.

Figure 6 ❧ Olmsted as an old man. After nearly four decades as the country's premier landscape architect, Olmsted retired in 1895. During that fruitful career he had created approximately 300 plans. After his death in 1903, the Olmsted firm undertook more than 3,000 projects in the next half century.

❧ Photograph attributed to Bartlett F. Henney, Boston. Courtesy of the National Park Service, Frederick Law Olmsted National Historic Site

In the meantime, however, Vaux and Olmsted had also developed independent interests; therefore, in 1872 they amicably dissolved their firm and went in separate directions.

Olmsted Alone

As his fame spread, Olmsted found his skills in growing demand until eventually it became almost too much for him to handle. After leaving Vaux he went on to design Mountain View Cemetery, Oakland, Calif.; Mount Royal Park, Montreal, Canada; Yale University, New Haven, Conn.; the U.S. Capitol grounds, Washington, D.C.; Back Bay Fens, Boston; and, of course, Point Chautauqua, N.Y., among other sites. As the pressure of work increased, he took on assistants and apprentices. Among the many plans developed during this period were those for Stanford University, Palo Alto, Calif.; the Chicago World's Fair of 1893; the Biltmore Estate, Asheville, N. C.; and the National Zoological Park, Washington, D.C. By 1890 his firm had taken the name F. L. Olmsted & Co., and employed 20 people. After Olmsted's death in 1903, the firm continued under the direction of his son and undertook hundreds of projects across the country.

THE OLMSTED PRINCIPLES

*S*everal general concepts distilled out of his varied life experience guided Olmsted during his four decades of service as America's foremost landscape architect. These notions derived from the two complementary elements of his life philosophy: his deep love and respect for natural beauty, and his conviction that human society should be allowed to benefit from the ameliorative influences of nature. These fundamental ideas formed a clear set of guiding principles that found expression in all his creations:

1. Naturalness

Throughout his long career, Olmsted's dominant theme was naturalness. From earliest childhood he was imbued with a deep love and appreciation for natural beauty. Born and reared amidst the magnificent scenery of the Connecticut Valley, he spent much of his early life in the pursuit of nature, not only in his native New England but also in extensive travels to other parts of the world. His observations of a great variety of landscapes led to the conviction that natural beauty was superior to anything that human beings could conceive. Therefore, he consistently upheld nature as the supreme ideal in all his work, and he determinedly avoided all appearance of artificiality and geometric regularity.

2. Conforming a Design to the Natural Lay of the Land

Olmsted's profound respect for nature led him to base his designs upon the natural formation of the land. His plans creatively used the existing configuration of the terrain in ways that avoided distorting or imposing upon it a rigid, arbitrary design. Olmsted's parks and communities have therefore retained their natural beauty for all time – when not encroached upon by commercial interests or the misguided actions of residents. On those occasions when he encountered an uninteresting natural setting, as at Riverside, Illinois, Olmsted contrived to enhance the natural landscape in a manner that might lead one to believe that this is the way nature would have done it if only she had thought of it.

3. Creating Curvilinear Forms with Unexpected Vistas

In his early park planning and later as a planner of communities, Olmsted insisted that the roadways be gently curving, a principle that had originated with the English park designers. This was a clearly preferable alternative to the conventional grid system:

> The grid plan made narrow, poorly ventilated housing necessary, or at least profitable…The narrowness of these houses set down meanly side by side squeezed together for the highest profit from each block, enforced the wrong kind of building [Stevenson 1977, p. 328].

> [Olmsted] pierced through what had become custom. If one changed the street pattern and the spacing of houses, then all this dreary monotony might be broken up [Stevenson 1977, p. 329].

Olmsted relied upon these curving roadways to achieve the effect he termed "The Mystery." Because one never knew what lay around the next bend, the view that emerged became a refreshing surprise. The curves also accentuated the visual effect of an endlessly verdant scene.

His roadway designs also performed a social function dear to Olmsted – that of bringing the people of a community together. He configured these avenues in such a way that the inhabitants cannot avoid seeing and being aware of each other, because they are forced to walk or drive along the same routes. They must enter the community by a main arterial, and they have to follow a common access route to reach the recreational areas that all share.

4. Providing Central Common Lands That Bring People Together

Centrally located lawns, meadows, and woodlands are invariable features of Olmsted community designs. These are intended to offer congenial surroundings where like-minded people can meet and where diverse groups can see and become acquainted with each other. In combination with the roadway design, these common areas foster an Olmsted ideal of human relations he termed "communicativeness."

> [A] peculiar ideal that motivated his work was not a catchy one, appealing as it did to impulses too lofty to be comfortably, or often, indulged. He called it "communicativeness." ...Communicativeness involved recognizing, and acting consistently on the recognition, that one had an essential community of interest with other human beings, regardless of regional, class, economic, color, religious, or whatever differences. ...[Communicativeness] was democratic, and utopian [Stevenson 1977, p. xiv].

Olmsted believed not only that a well-designed landscape plan brings people together but also that the periodic review of a plan is vital to the good of the people who live in the community. Completed projects that are not evaluated and reviewed as part of the environment are doomed to become dead monuments. He further maintained that all community planning must be thought of in relationship to the past. Not knowing about past achievements and failures can result in expensive errors.

5. Creating a Restful Sylvan Retreat from the Crowded City

Olmsted wished that his designs might provide places where people could recover from the crowded conditions and stresses of working in cities.

> Without recuperation and recreation of force, the power of each individual to labor wisely and honestly is soon lost …But to this process of recuperation a condition is necessary, known since the days of Aesop as the unbending of the faculties which have been tasked…by the occupation of the imagination with objects and reflections of a quite different character from those which are associated with their bent condition.[4]

Like many others of his time, Olmsted believed that cities are the great instruments of civilization, and that planned communities need to be connected to cities. But he also knew that people need to be released from the high energy of urban places at times and to have a chance to rest in peaceful, natural surroundings. To maintain such an atmosphere, he stressed that houses should not "elbow" each other across lawns but should have plenty of lawn space around them. "A small space, it should not be forgotten, may serve to present a choice refreshment to a city, provided the circumstances are favorable for an extended outlook upon natural elements of scenery" [from a letter by Olmsted to *The Century Magazine* of October 1886].

[4] From Olmsted's Preliminary Report…for the Laying Out of a Park in Brooklyn, N.Y. (1866), quoted in Stevenson 1977, p. 282.

OLMSTED'S WORK IN PERSPECTIVE

*S*ome observers, notably Albert Fein, have suggested that Olmsted's planning career can be divided into two distinct but somewhat overlapping periods [Fein 1972, p. 5]. Fein suggests that during the first of these periods Olmsted found employment that gave him freedom to pursue his idealistic aims. According to this view, the later period found Olmsted, to his discomfort, constrained by conditions imposed by the brash new class of industrialists and financiers that came to ascendancy during the latter part of the century.

> The two major urban accomplishments that mark the start and the conclusion of Olmsted's career as an environmental planner – Central Park and the Chicago World's Fair [of 1893] – were prompted by two different patrons, two different sets of social conditions and two different national and urban ideals, resulting in sharply contrasting environmental forms. While both designs reflect thoughtful and careful attention to scientific and technical matters, they are, in aesthetic and cultural terms, almost antithetical [Fein 1972, p. 7].

Other scholars disagree with Fein's twofold division of Olmsted's career, insisting that insufficient evidence can be found for such an attitudinal change. If any such differences existed between these two eras in Olmsted's professional life, these could be explained in part by the changing nature of his business. Rather than any lessening of Olmsted's ideals, more likely they reflected a certain pragmatism dictated by the necessity of obtaining commissions from commercial developers during those later years when he felt responsible for maintaining the financial viability of his firm. Earlier, when working alone or in partnership with Vaux, he was able to insist firmly upon adherence to his principles, as indeed he did most emphatically while negotiating with the founders of Point Chautauqua.

Even in this early period, much depended upon the power of Olmsted's bargaining position. At Point Chautauqua he was negotiating from strength; this was less true in some other cases. In particular, it should be noted that Olmsted's experience in implementing the Greensward design for Central Park was somewhat less congenial than is sometimes suggested. Indeed, the record discloses that at Central Park he encountered considerable conflict in a politically charged situation and was forced to make compromises before the project was completed. Nevertheless, it should be emphasized that, throughout his career, Olmsted's work preserved certain important constants. Especially in his park designs, he adhered to a naturalistic, almost romantic style; and he was always concerned that his creations be consistent with local climatic and site conditions. With these cautions, however, it seems useful to assess Olmsted's work broadly within these two time frames.

The Early Period

The first phase of Olmsted's planning career began in 1858, when the Olmsted-Vaux plan for Central Park was accepted, and continued until about 1878. During these early years he worked with public officials, community builders who believed in the importance of planning and who, with notable exceptions, left him relatively free to develop his own ideas. This period saw many of his greatest achievements: Central Park; the College at Berkeley, California; Yosemite National Park; the community at Riverside, Illinois; and parks in Brooklyn, Chicago, Buffalo, Boston, and Montreal.

In these early years Olmsted was relatively free to adapt his designs to the land; he did not have to be as concerned with accommodating to large, overpowering buildings or structures as later proved to be the case. For the most part, the people who hired him at this time were influenced by a politically strong, idealistic elite, among whom were Unitarians and adherents to other liberal forms of Protestant theology. These included such figures as Horace Greeley, William Cullen Bryant, Henry Whitney Bellows, and Charles Loring Brace, founder of the Children's Aid Society. The Transcendentalism of Ralph Waldo Emerson was important to these people.

The Later Period

In subsequent years – from 1878 to his retirement in 1895 – his plans came increasingly under pressure from the private individuals, often members of the new industrialist class, who engaged his services but did not necessarily share his social goals. He found it necessary also to cooperate with architects of the new, imposing, chateau-like buildings and houses that came into favor at the time. The doctrine of Social Darwinism, "the survival of the fittest," held sway in this period. Society was divided more or less into two classes: those who succeeded and those who failed.

At this time the entrances to Central Park were fitted with majestic new gates, made to conform with the large houses being erected beside the park. Other Olmsted plans of this period included Biltmore, the estate of George Vanderbilt at Asheville, North Carolina; the college campus at Stanford; and some notable parks, such as those in Boston. Curving roads and streets continued to make their appearance in the new communities designed by Olmsted. Most of these plans, however, were subject to constraints imposed by land developers, who commonly allocated little or no internal space to parkland – land that could be enjoyed by all inhabitants of the place. Instead, developers often set these new communities next to public park areas, thus enabling them to offer such amenities to property buyers at no cost to themselves.

Two Examples

The contrasting characteristics of Olmsted designs from these periods are well illustrated by the plans he drew up for two university campuses in California: the earlier one at Berkeley and the later one at Stanford. His plan for Berkeley is picturesque and small in scale, with buildings scattered throughout the grounds. The Stanford plan is perfectly symmetrical, having been made to conform to the demands of Leland Stanford, who had commissioned the plan in memory of his son. Among his specifications was the requirement that buildings be placed at the center, on a plane so that no "topographical difficulties need ever stand in the way of setting other buildings as they may in the future...be found desirable" [Fein 1972]. The Stanford design is reminiscent of the rigid symmetry of the French garden plans, representing the concept that Capability Brown had defeated. Olmsted found little pleasure in having to work under constraints of this nature.

THE OLMSTED HERITAGE

*T*he lasting consequences of Olmsted's crowded career are everywhere to be seen. Many eminent designers, both during his own time and later, have acknowledged their immense debt to Olmsted and his ideas. These concepts were responsible for generating important new trends in community design, which have since spread throughout the world. No less significant are the enduring material monuments that Olmsted left behind or the pleasure of those people who continue to enjoy the tranquil environments he created for them.

Effects on Architecture and Design

In a variety of ways Olmsted influenced later generations of designers. Prominent among these was the architect Frank Lloyd Wright, who positioned his houses, as Olmsted had placed parks, on the natural landscape, in ways that would not destroy or detract from its natural look. Wright used building materials from the surrounding locality. He placed gardens inside his houses and filled them with flowers and plants native to the environment. "Frederick Law Olmsted and Ebenezer Howard brought the garden into the city; Wright brought it into the home itself" [Miller 1989, p. 86].

Olmsted and his partner, Calvert Vaux, developed for Central Park a system of aesthetically designed grade separations – underpasses and overpasses that ingeniously shield the park from city traffic. In the years since, grade separations of this kind have become a standard device for highway engineers. It is ironic that one of Olmsted's most beautiful designs, Delaware Park in Buffalo, has been marred by the replacement of its charming Humbolt Parkway with a superhighway.

New Directions for Urban and Regional Planning

Building upon Olmsted's concepts, a number of eminent designers have launched major innovations in community and regional planning. One such person was Ebenezer Howard (1850-1928), the English urban planner, who was deeply influenced by the Olmsted community Riverside. This became the inspiration for Howard's Garden City idea. Garden cities are planned, self-sufficient communities built outside a metropolis in empty terrain and surrounded by uninhabited parkland called a Greenbelt. They are connected to the outside world by railways and good roads. The usual garden city design calls for curving streets and allocates space for shops, parks, churches, playgrounds, recreation fields, industry, village greens. A village council provides governance and arranges for social activities. It was Howard's idea that people would want to live in these small cities instead of crowding into large cities.

After World War II the popular New Towns of Britain and the Continent were built to relieve overcrowding in the major cities. These New Towns used many of the planning principles of the garden city. In Europe New Towns have had a significant place in the plans for Copenhagen, Helsinki, Stockholm, and Paris. In Third World countries, planned cities of this kind are integral parts of economic development programs and include a number of new capital cities.

The New Towns of Britain form a ring 25 to 30 miles from the center of London and are surrounded by Greenbelts designed to prevent the towns from simply growing out along the highways. Invariably, parks occupy a prominent place in such communities, and roadways are curved [Stamp and Beaver, pp. 630-631]. A good example of such a community is Crawley New Town, which began as a largely working-class village. It has many trees and rolling lawns similar to those of the large English estates [Commission for the New Towns 1961]. The general feeling is one of which Olmsted would have heartily approved.

In the United States, Ebenezer Howard's Garden City idea was applied at Sunnyside Gardens by planners Henry Wright and Clarence Stein, who had been active in developing lower-cost housing. The two also planned the classic community project of Radburn, which employs the Olmsted-Vaux idea of grade separations for different types of traffic.

The New Town idea has not been as popular in America as in Europe, where it has been used extensively. Here it has been hard to overcome the grid-pattern habit and the inclination of towns simply to grow outward along highways. Rarely does a planner take a large tract of land, separated by distance from the city, and create within it a community provided with adequate parkland and a means to prevent building construction along bypass roads. But it is interesting that Britain, the country that provided Olmsted's initial inspiration, should take back, with enthusiasm, Olmsted ideas as illustrated by the work of Ebenezer Howard.

Enduring Monuments to Olmsted's Work

In association with Vaux, and later working alone and through his firm of landscape architects, Olmsted proved to be a prolific planner of parks, community designs, college and university campuses, and private estates. From New England to California, hundreds of his creations remain as testimonials to the enduring qualities of his ideas. Among the best known and most intensively used and enjoyed of these are his great public parks, notably Central Park in New York, Prospect Park in Brooklyn, and Delaware Park in Buffalo. But some observers consider his community plans to be the most innovative and influential of his works, because they gave rise to the worldwide movements described earlier.

23

Riverside, Illinois, was the first successful community design of Olmsted's career, and some believe it to be his best. Located on the Des Plaines River about twenty miles from Chicago, on a 1,600-acre tract that was at that time still separate from the city, it began on completely empty, desolate terrain, flat except for land that rose slightly along the riverbanks. Planning a community for an entirely empty expanse of land was a revolutionary idea at that time. It had been done for such religious communities as Brook Farm, Oneida, and Red Bank. But Riverside was secular – as was Llewellyn, the first planned community in America, which set a precedent and served to some extent as a model for Olmsted as he began work. The designer of Llewellyn, Alexander Jackson Davis, had been an early influence on Olmsted. Davis was a close friend of Downing, Olmsted's main mentor. And, as Calvert Vaux, who was working with Olmsted at Riverside, had been Downing's assistant during the development of Llewellyn Park, Olmsted could draw upon Vaux's experience.

Here at Riverside in 1868, Olmsted put in place the same curving roadways he had used in his park designs [Figure 7]. As he described in his *Preliminary Report Upon The Proposed Suburban Village At Riverside, Near Chicago*, they should have "gracefully curved lines, generous spaces, and the absence of sharp corners, the idea being to suggest and imply leisure, contemplativeness and happy tranquility" [Fein 1972, p. 35].

Olmsted wanted the layout of Riverside to encourage communal activities, so he planned for the houses to be built around village-green-like areas that incorporated commons and playgrounds. Connecting these commons were drives and walkways. The drives were "good hard roads," well-lighted by street lamps. "Families dwelling within a suburb [would] enjoy much in common, and all the more enjoy it because it is in common" [Fein 1972, p. 35].

The Des Plaines River was the most prominent physical feature, and Olmsted organized the community in such a way as to give it importance. The river was in the center of the plan, and public space – parks – were placed along it. Land here was flat and thus did not lend itself, in the Olmsted view, to a picturesque treatment with range and views. Hence he concentrated on trees and grass – green overhead and underfoot.

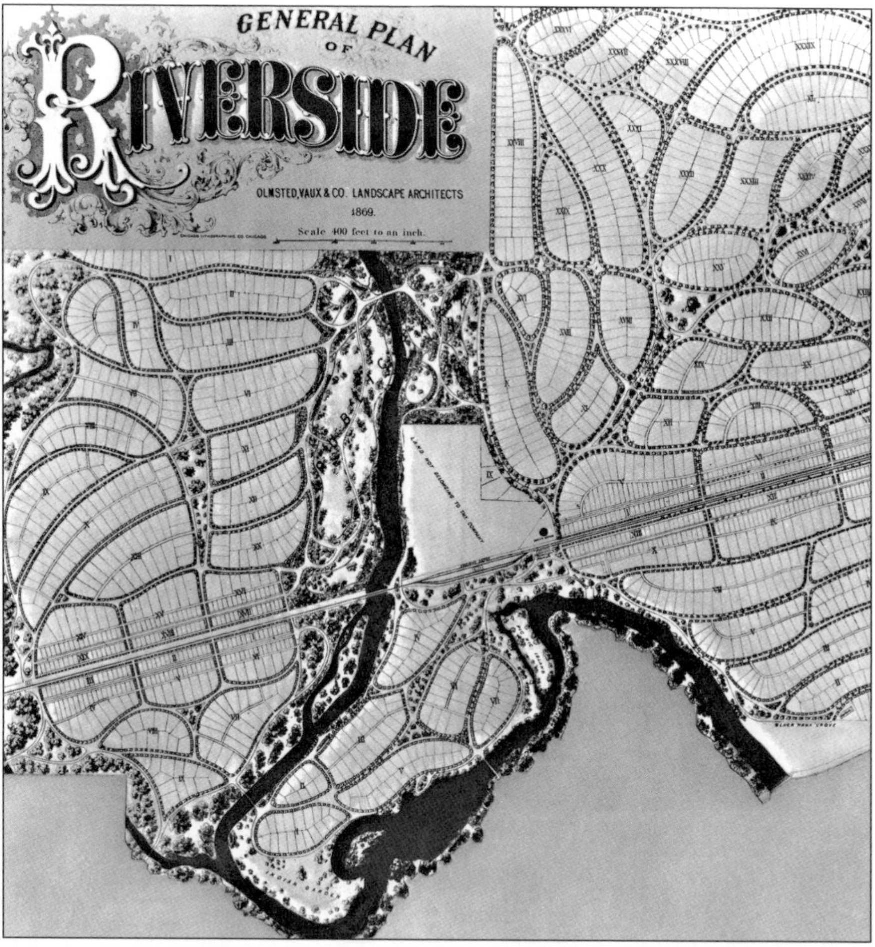

Figure 7 ❧ General plan of Riverside, Illinois, Olmsted, Vaux & Co. Landscape Architects, 1869. The planning of a residential suburb on 1,600 acres of nearly flat land near Chicago presented Olmsted and Vaux with a unique challenge. Their solution was to organize the community around the only prominent physical feature, the Des Plaines River, which ran through the area. Along the riverbanks they placed parks and public spaces with an abundance of trees and broad, grassy areas, and in the residential areas they provided for large building lots to ensure plentiful green spaces. Throughout the community, tree-lined, curving roadways of the kind previously used by Olmsted and Vaux in their park designs contrived an atmosphere of relaxation and tranquility.

❧ Chicago Lithographing Co., Chicago, n.d. Courtesy of the National Park Service, Frederick Law Olmsted National Historic Site

What is of importance in the planning of Riverside is the prevalence of public land – parkland that "families dwelling within a suburb [would] enjoy… in common." This open space amounted to 1,600 acres – two and a half square miles. It consisted of the commons, playgrounds, and public walks and drives along the river. Few developers today give over such a generous portion of land to public lands *within* a planned community. Even in the subsequent designs of Olmsted, such as Tarrytown Heights in 1871 and Parkside in Buffalo in 1872, public land was either not extensive or the community was added to an already existing park. (Note, too, that in each of these cases, Olmsted was forced, reluctantly, to work with land that was either flat or only gently rolling).

Riverside is unique in that it is the first time a *landscape* architect was in charge of designing a real estate project [Newton 1971, p. 468]. It was also one of the few times Olmsted's ideas for a planned community were carried out almost in their entirety. The highway that he was convinced should connect Riverside with the center of Chicago was never put in place, but nearly everything else was. Today the community remains intact, zealously defended by its inhabitants while the metropolis changes all around it.

On one occasion when Olmsted received an opportunity to work with site conditions of the kind he found most challenging, the design was never built. In 1873 he was asked to submit a plan for the expansion of the village of Tacoma, Washington. The Northern Pacific Railroad Company had just selected it as its western terminus. The land was on the edge of a bay off of Puget Sound, which afforded a protected deepwater anchorage but also presented a difficult sloping terrain. Olmsted developed an imaginative plan that accommodated the street layout to the contours of the land. However, Olmsted's plan produced consternation in the railway company's offices as well as in the village of Tacoma: it did not follow the traditional grid pattern! The company rejected the Olmsted plan in favor of a conventional grid pattern produced by others.

One individual expressed local reaction to Olmsted's magnificent plan this way: "The most fantastic plat of a town that was ever seen. There wasn't a straight line, a right angle or a corner lot. The blocks were shaped like melons, pears, and sweet potatoes. One block, shaped like a banana" [Quoted in Rybczynski 1999, p. 329]. Nonetheless, as we shall see, Olmsted's unrealized Tacoma design contained the seed for his plan for Point Chautauqua.

The Olmsted Spirit of Community

Communities with good designs endure, and many of Olmsted's have survived for well over a century. Their inhabitants are proud of them and enthusiastic about them, and they protect them with intense zeal. Their ardent attachment to their communities persists generation after generation. With much pleasure they tell stories of the ancestors who first occupied their houses and those who followed. There may be many reasons for this – attachments to friends and associations that go back many years, the sense of closeness to nature inherent to Olmsted designs, the feelings of seclusion and sanctuary.

> In the machine age it is important in some way perhaps immeasurable by the sciences of biology and psychology, but nonetheless real, for man to confirm with his senses that he lives in a world of seasonal rhythms – of vernal buds, falling leaves, drifting snow. Olmsted knew this. His parks are more than charming exercises in a quaint, outmoded style known as the picturesque. They are still perhaps more than ever, a therapeutic, life-enhancing force and for this reason they should be allowed to endure [Barlow and Alex 1972, p. 51].

An Olmsted community that has lasted has a certain feeling about it. Fletcher Steele, a landscape architect who was one of Olmsted's students, explained the reason for this. He said that Olmsted was an "extraordinary genius" who had "unusual refinement of feeling for everything he touched (refinement meaning feeling for exquisite finish and consideration of the more intimate if generally unexpressed needs of people)" [quoted in Karson 1989, p. 16].

For those who turned to him for the planning of their parks and residential communities, Olmsted was a great teacher. His clients came mainly from the elite of his day, who readily adopted his principles. The position of leadership enjoyed by these people further magnified the wide acceptance of Olmsted's ideals and outlook. In philosophy and influence, he belonged to a distinguished group of nineteenth-century artistic figures:

> [These individuals created] a romantic tradition, which encouraged what one might call a compulsory love of nature – and this nature is of a variety seen through the eyes of a limited number of artists. Corot and the Barbison school among painters, Frederick Law Olmsted and Charles Eliot among landscape architects…were enormously influential in forming the definite traditions of the leisure class [quoted in Karson 1989, p. 317].

Olmsted's influence on the group that engaged him to design Point Chautauqua was of this sort. His ideals prevailed over the preconceived notions of these first leaders, and the Olmsted principles incorporated in his plan for Point Chautauqua have left a lasting imprint on the spirit of the community and on the visual impact of its winding roadways and charming vistas. Here is preserved that distinctive feeling which is common to Olmsted-designed places.

CHAPTER ❧ THREE
Olmsted's Only Religious
═══════════Community

*F*rederick Law Olmsted planned the layout of Point Chautauqua's roads, lots, and public spaces in 1875, working alone, no longer in association with his earlier partner, Vaux. The Point Chautauqua plan is a direct lineal descendant of his earlier design for Riverside and, in particular, of his aborted plan for Tacoma, Washington – but with some significant differences. Despite its unique aspects, however, the Point Chautauqua design faithfully embodies Olmsted's principles. These are apparent 125 years later, despite the changes that time has brought to the community.

In some measure the Point Chautauqua of today is a museum for the several cultural eras through which it has passed during the century and a quarter since its founding. The most distinctive artifacts remaining from those evolutionary stages are its houses; each time period left a residue of architectural styles representative of that day. Yet it is the Victorian structures built by Point Chautauqua's earliest residents that convey the essence of the settlement and leave the most lasting impression upon visitors. Throughout the long progression of this community, however, the road and lot systems have endured very much as the master directed, and the outlines of his public spaces have remained largely in place.

29
❧

RELIGIOUS COLONY

*I*n its transformation over the years from a church camp to the residential community it is today, Point Chautauqua has in many ways mirrored the broader societal and economic trends taking place in the country at large. Yet, to a significant degree, the changes at Point Chautauqua have also followed shifts in this community's purpose and functions and in the makeup of its population. Considering the extent of these changes and the time that has passed since Olmsted prepared his plan, the physical form of that design has been remarkably persistent – as has the sense of natural beauty and tranquility that it imparts. That form preserves two essential elements of the initial plan: the manifest expressions of Olmsted's principles of design, aesthetics, and social interaction; and the relics of the settlement's original religious mission.

Olmsted and the Baptists

In former times Lake Chautauqua was ringed by Bible camps, and several of these remain today. They are remnants of that extraordinary event in early American cultural history known as the "Great Awakening," a revival of religious fervor that swept through the colonies during the eighteenth century and rekindled with still greater intensity during the first half of the nineteenth century. The principal agents for the spread of this zeal were itinerant preachers, evangelists who conducted revival camp meetings throughout what was then the western frontier. It was predominantly a Protestant phenomenon, led especially by Methodists and Baptists [Sweet 1944, 1946; Weisberger 1958].

These revival meetings – great "wilderness festivals" – convened each summer at campgrounds devoted to the purpose. The nature of these "sacred other places" drew upon biblical precedents, especially the Hebrew Feast of Tabernacles. Conspicuous on the grounds were massive wooden structures that, indeed, were called "tabernacles": "great, roofed sheds…large enough to shelter the preacher's stand and the entire audience" [Weiss 1987, p. 14]. Other physical features of biblical origin were the sacred "groves" – wooded areas used for religious retreats – and the "tents" (in reference to the dwellings of the nomadic Hebrew tribes) – small family residences that, in fact, were often constructed of wooden slabs. Organizers of these outdoor gatherings emphasized their health benefits and recreational value, which today would be called the "psychic benefits of nature immersions" [Weiss 1987, p. 144].

Of the campgrounds on the shores of Lake Chautauqua in the 1870s, the most prominent were the Baptist camp at Point Chautauqua on the eastern side of the lake, and the Methodist camp, called the Chautauqua Assembly Ground, at Fair Point on the opposite shore.[5] Of the two, Chautauqua Assembly (later to become Chautauqua Institution) was the earlier and, ultimately, the more successful as a religious venture.[6]

Encouraged by the immediate popularity enjoyed by the Chautauqua Assembly (also referred to as the Chautauqua Lake Camp Meeting Grounds), which had opened in 1872, leaders of the American Baptist Church determined to establish a similar operation on the opposite shore of the lake. The site chosen was at Leet's Point, on land that had been purchased by Captain Anson Leet in 1817 from the Holland Land Company. From Leet's descendants, the Baptists in 1875 bought 106 acres, largely hillside and heavily wooded, sloping down to Chautauqua Lake, and renamed it Point Chautauqua. A joint-stock company, the Point Chautauqua Association, was then formed with "a Board of Fifteen Directors, two-thirds of whom must be members of regular Baptist Churches in good standing" [Leet 1957, p. 3].

The newly formed Point Chautauqua Association thereupon approached Frederick Law Olmsted with a proposal that he develop a plan for the layout

31

---

[5]   Records of the time also mention a Congregationalist camp at Lake View, near present-day Jamestown [Leet 1957, p. 2].

[6]   The Chautauqua Institution is on the National Register and has been declared a National Historic Landmark. Begun as a Sunday-school camp for Methodists, it has continued to support a degree of religious activity in its summer program, though in later years this has become increasingly ecumenical in nature. At a very early date Chautauqua Institution developed an educational and cultural program that has earned world renown.

of Point Chautauqua's grounds. Olmsted had been working since 1868 on a master plan for Buffalo's city parks and a number of other development projects in that city, and he agreed to meet with members of the Point Chautauqua Board to consider their undertaking. In October 1875, following a conference with Buffalo leaders, Olmsted journeyed to Chautauqua Lake, where he visited the Chautauqua Lake Camp Grounds at Fair Point and then inspected the Point Chautauqua site.

Meeting afterward with the Baptist group in Mayville, Olmsted listened to their ideas for the layout of their grounds. Olmsted then shared with them his observations of Fair Point and urged a very different kind of plan for Point Chautauqua. In a subsequent letter to the President of the Point Chautauqua Association, he set down in writing his views on this subject.[7] In answer to the directors' desire that Point Chautauqua's grounds be designed along lines similar to those at Fair Point, Olmsted declared that he found the Chautauqua Lake Camp Meeting Grounds to be overcrowded, that insufficient attention was being paid to sanitation and water supply, and that sunlight was lacking because of the continuous tree cover. This was definitely not a model for Point Chautauqua's grounds. Olmsted's conception of Point Chautauqua was that it should be a summer city with ample sanitation; ample water supply; ample space, trees, shrubs, and flowers; and ample locations for the enjoyment of views ("prospects," in the language of the 1870s). Following his October meeting with the directors, Olmsted returned to New York City and began the planning of Point Chautauqua.

The Olmsted Design

In preparing the Point Chautauqua design, Olmsted looked to two earlier works for precedents. The first was the widely acclaimed 1868 plan for Riverside, Illinois, and the second was his superb but rejected 1873 layout for Tacoma, Washington. As at Riverside, Olmsted was directly concerned with

32

---

[7] See Olmsted's letter of October 9, 1875, to Walter Sessions, Board President, who had been unable to attend the initial meeting in Mayville. Olmsted's caustic description of the conditions he found at Fair Point (Chautauqua Lake Camp Meeting Grounds), and his proposed alternatives to these, offer revealing insights into his philosophy of landscape design.

the configuration of Point Chautauqua's roadway and lot systems and their relationships to the lay of the land and to a body of water. Also, as at Riverside, Olmsted offered no specifications concerning the design or character of the residences and other structures to be built at Point Chautauqua. Nevertheless, Olmsted clearly preferred the natural conditions he found on the shores of Lake Chautauqua to those he had encountered in Illinois.

Despite the generally acknowledged success of his Riverside design, Olmsted is known to have been dissatisfied with the physical environment with which he had to work at that location. The landscape that constituted his raw material was flat and swampy, and it is a tribute to his ingenuity that he was able to create an extraordinarily attractive product from such unpromising topography:

> Riverside's novelty is that it was designed as a self-contained community from the start. Since there were no heights to climb from which to obtain lengthy vistas, the containment was likewise modest and monochromatic, and smaller dramas such as boating and driving were featured for inside the community. Everything worked for proximity. The impression of dwelling beneath a green cloud of foliage to protect the premises from the brightness of the prairie sky was carefully cultivated. The slow rhythmic turns of the roads meant that the inner space of the 1,600 acres might appear to be infinitely varied. So the ambience achieved the maximum effect with the minimal means of foliage and curving roads [Creese 1985, p. 220].

33

The natural conditions that Olmsted clearly preferred were those that offered hilly terrain adjacent to water. These he found at Tacoma, Washington, when he was asked in 1873 to prepare a design for that community. As described above, Tacoma climbs a steep hillside from the shores of an adjacent waterway. Those who commissioned the Tacoma plan found Olmsted's ideas

34

Figure 8 ❧ Olmsted's 1873 plan for Tacoma, Washington. When asked to develop a design for the village of Tacoma, Olmsted discovered there the site conditions that he regarded most interesting and challenging: land that sloped steeply down to the shores of an embayment of Puget Sound. He proceeded to lay out curving streets that conformed to the contour of the land, providing them with gentle gradients suitable for easy movement of pedestrians and horse-drawn vehicles. Tacoma officials summarily rejected Olmsted's innovative scheme because it failed to conform with the conventional grid pattern they had expected. The scheme developed by Olmsted for Tacoma did not go to waste, however; his imaginative solution for steep terrain proved valuable two years later when he encountered similar slope conditions at Point Chautauqua. Later generations of landscape architects have continued to follow this example. ❧ Courtesy of the National Park Service, Frederick Law Olmsted National Historic Site

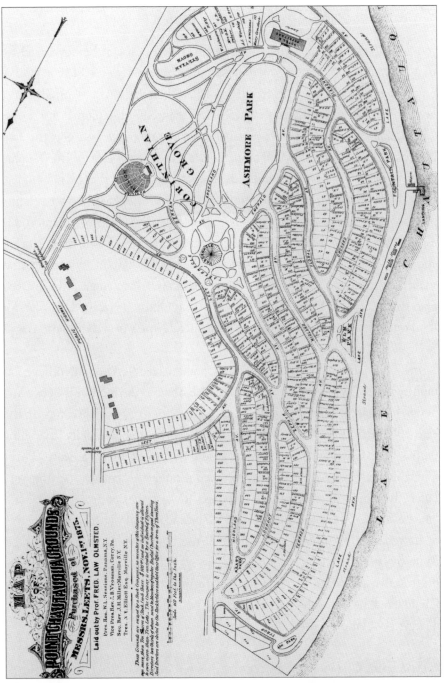

Figure 9 ❧ The 1875 Olmsted design for Point Chautauqua. The resemblance between Olmsted's street layout for Point Chautauqua and that of his rejected plan for Tacoma (Figure 8) is inescapable. The lovely tree-covered hillsides at Point Chautauqua provided him with the opportunity to test his earlier ideas in a perfect setting. The availability of the ready-made Tacoma design no doubt helps to explain the remarkable speed with which Olmsted was able to draft his Point Chautauqua plan after receiving the base map from local surveyor Tennant.

too advanced for their conservative tastes, but the design he developed for that community remains a superb example of his creative use of that kind of natural landscape he most favored [Figure 8]. A comparison of Olmsted's street layout for Tacoma with that which he prepared subsequently for Point Chautauqua [Figure 9] shows a remarkable resemblance between the two designs. This is especially apparent in the lower left sector of the Tacoma street layout, which is very similar in character to that of Point Chautauqua. In each situation, the salient features are the curvilinear roadways ascending steep slopes at angles that permit gradients sufficiently gentle for a comfortable ascent by pedestrians and horse-drawn vehicles, as well as the provision for centrally located parklands. So close are these two designs in appearance that some have speculated that Olmsted's design for Point Chautauqua is the Tacoma plan that was never built. What is clear is that Olmsted prepared the plan for the Point with remarkable speed, as if he already knew exactly what to do.

In several particulars, however, Point Chautauqua differs from his other community plans. With respect to Tacoma, the obvious distinction is between a design for a major railway terminus and a design for a rustic Bible camp. In the case of Riverside, the intention was to create a suburb of a rapidly expanding metropolis, Chicago, to which it would be linked by a railway. Point Chautauqua, on the other hand, occupied a rural site that was far from any large city – and still is today. Nevertheless, it was to be connected by rail and lake steamer to Pittsburgh, Buffalo, and Cleveland, which were the main sources of its vacationing inhabitants. In time, the older modes of transportation came to be replaced by modern expressways, which tie it to each of those metropolises. Being so far removed from such places, however, Point Chautauqua has never had to consider the possibility of becoming enclosed by a larger population center.

The Point Chautauqua project also differed from Riverside in other ways. For one thing, the rail line serving Riverside bisected the community, necessitating a modified grid street pattern in the blocks adjacent to it. Point Chautauqua suffered from no such constraints, and Olmsted thus had free rein to construct the curvilinear pattern he always preferred. Another distinction between the two projects was the degree of Olmsted's direct involvement. Olmsted, Vaux & Co. were able to assume a greater role in the details of Riverside's planning, for instance, specifying that the river be dammed for recreational purposes and directing the planting of many thousands of trees and shrubs. Later, working alone, Olmsted was under much pressure from other, larger projects then under way, notably the Buffalo park system. He was therefore unable to give close attention to the minute particulars of the Point Chautauqua project.

In still one other respect the Point Chautauqua plan was truly exceptional. Olmsted's original commission was for a religious community, the only one he ever designed. Precedents for this sort of planned religious community existed at Brook Farm and a number of other sites, but Olmsted undertook such an assignment only in this instance. The most conspicuous effect of this initial purpose, as might be expected, was the large amount of space allocated to religious functions, especially the Tabernacle grounds and such outdoor meeting places as the Corinthian Grove.

The Baptist Camp
In February 1876 Olmsted forwarded his new design. This was greeted with enthusiasm, as Point Chautauqua Association Secretary Miller's letter of acknowledgement indicates:

> Map recd. today. Absence from home has prevented my writing with reference to the beautiful map of Point Chaut. we received from you about three weeks ago. We are well pleased with it.[8]

37

[8]   Letter from J. H. Miller to Frederick Law Olmsted, March 28, 1876.

Implementation of the Olmsted plan began shortly thereafter. An 1876 article in the *Jamestown Journal* describes what followed:

> During the past summer, Fred Law Olmsted, who planned Central Park, New York, has laid out Chautauqua Point, into winding avenues twenty-six feet wide, enclosing four hundred and sixty-five lots, of one-eighth of an acre each. From low water mark at the extreme westerly point of the cape to the eastern bounds of the Point is about half a mile, with an elevation of one hundred and five feet. The entire Point embraces one hundred acres, fifteen of which is comprised in a grove lying upon the south side and overlooking Dewittville Bay. In the years to come thousands will bless the name of Capt. Leet, who so jealously guarded this beautiful woodland grove with its great variety of graceful trees, among which may be mentioned the sugar maple, the oak, the chestnut, the butternut, the beech and the water willow. Eight beautiful springs afford an abundance of pure cold water, and the summer breeze that invariably plays over and around the Point is always refreshing to the visitor [quoted in Leet 1957, p. 3].

Olmsted placed the public portion of Point Chautauqua on that part of the land with the gentlest slope. At the highest point he located the two assembly areas: the Tabernacle (enclosed) and the Pavilion (open air). Sloping downhill from the assembly areas were parklands: the Corinthian and Sylvan Groves – tree-covered and laced with walks – and Ashmore Park – open, and bordered with a walk. At the foot of Ashmore Park was a plot designated for a small hotel and refectory. Lake Avenue bordered the lakefront, and the grounds lying between this street and the lakeshore (called The Strand) were public, occupied only by two docks to accommodate the lake steamboats. The remainder was reserved for community recreational use.

The private portion of the grounds occupied the more steeply inclined land, with a slope as much as 12 to 100. Olmsted laid out the streets so that they had a pedestrian- and carriage-comfortable slope of 1 to 20. The blocks were long, narrow, and gently curvilinear. The only landscaping recommendation by Olmsted was for the planting of trees on the fill side of the streets, as a way of stabilizing the newly placed soil. Earth ditches lined the streets to channel storm water downward into the lake.

Immediately following its delivery, Olmsted's design was surveyed and staked out by M. D. Tennant of nearby Westfield. Shortly afterward, the roadways were graded and graveled, and the parklands developed:

> There is of the reserve for the public use a grove containing some twenty acres; and it is a beautiful grove; no building to be in the grove except the Auditorium. Next is the Grand Park [Ashmore Park] or camping grounds, where all tents will be pitched by those wishing to live in tents…There are also several minor parks. The one at the boat landing has two fountains now in full play, fed by springs from the higher grounds. There are some six or eight good permanent springs of soft water, and four of them have pumps in them ready for the use of the thirsty sojourner on a hot day – one with a rustic bower or arbor inviting the stranger to take a seat beneath its cooling shade [Ward 1876].

Further consultation with Olmsted by Point Chautauqua's directors continued as the work progressed:

> Our grounds are now being worked. We are well pleased with the general plan. Our property is increasing in value. I will solicit your advice on certain points with which I am not perfectly familiar.[9]

[9] Letter to Olmsted from J. H. Miller dated June 5, 1876.

Figure 10 ❧ The Hartson Tabernacle. In keeping with the religious mission of Point Chautauqua's Baptist founders, this imposing house of worship commanded the highest ground in the settlement, towering over the houses and tents of the faithful arranged along the slopes below. Completed in December 1879 and designed to seat an audience of 5,000, the Tabernacle was 190 feet long and 150 feet wide and was topped by a 134-foot spire. In this 1890 photograph the grand edifice seems to impart an otherworldly atmosphere, even though its religious function had ceased years earlier.   ❧ Courtesy of the Fenton Historical Society

That first summer also saw construction of a dock for steamboats, with a store building at the land end of the dock. Olmsted's prior advice on this project reveals his firm ideas on the importance of good transport connections, as well as his continual desire to promote social interaction:

> All points in doubt respecting the wharf seem to turn upon local questions of economy rather than general design, and on these my judgment would be of no value to you. I think that if it could be afforded all the dimensions would be better much larger and that a prettily designed shelter on the outer block, such as would be suitable for a small railway station, would be not only a convenience but make the wharf an agreeable resort when no boats were coming to it and give a pleasanter first impression to people arriving than they would obtain from a wharf which was nothing more than an ordinary convenience or bare necessity.[10]

[10]   Letter from Olmsted to Miller, January 18, 1876.

Figure 11 ❧ The Grand Hotel. Though religious instruction was the prime purpose for the founding of Point Chautauqua, a commercial motive quickly emerged when the Association decided to construct an immense luxury establishment to be called, appropriately, the Grand Hotel. In a space near the Tabernacle that had originally been intended for Olmsted's Ashmore Park, this elaborate multi-story structure was built to accommodate 400 guests, making it by far the largest and fanciest hostelry in the region. Because of its great size and hilltop location, the Grand Hotel loomed over the upper basin of Lake Chautauqua. Later sold to commercial interests, the hotel apparently was never profitable. In 1902 it was destroyed in a spectacular fire. A court later convicted one of its owners of deliberately setting the fire in an effort to collect insurance. ❧ Photograph courtesy of Helen Campbell

41
❧

Figure 12 ❧ Lobby and sitting room of the Grand Hotel, 1895. Throughout the Chautauqua region the Grand Hotel was renowned not only for its great size but also for the splendor of its interior and the richness of its appointments. These featured solid black walnut furniture, sumptuous carpeting, expensive china and silverware, and other finery intended for the comfort of guests. The dramatic fire that demolished the structure early on the morning of October 17, 1902, spared none of these. Even today, owners of houses occupying the former hotel site occasionally unearth shards of pottery and pieces of silverware bearing the Grand Hotel mark.

❧ Courtesy of the Fenton Historical Society

Located on the shore opposite the intersection of Lake and Diamond Avenues and across from Fountain Park, the dock was 106 feet in length and 24 feet in width, with an ell 80 feet in length. It was to be "by far the finest dock on the lake." The contract price was $1,900.

In 1878 construction commenced on what was to be called the Hartson Tabernacle, using timbers already on the grounds, and was completed by December of the following year. Built to seat 5,000 people and set on one of the higher parts of the grounds, the Tabernacle was an imposing structure, 190 feet long and 150 feet wide, with a tower rising 134 feet from the ground to the top of the spire [Figure 10]. In pictures of the period it stands well above the surrounding trees and houses and is visible from far out into the lake.

Also in 1878, the Point Chautauqua Association contracted for construction of a Point Chautauqua Hotel. Originally the hotel was to have been located on the south side of Diamond Avenue, opposite the lower end of Ashmore Park. When construction started, the building was shifted to the center of the park. Later renamed the Grand Hotel, it was much larger than originally intended. The main building was a multi-story structure 250 feet long by 45 feet wide, with a center pavilion 52 by 30 feet in front. The dining hall and culinary department were 144 by 60 feet, running back at right angles to the main building. The center tower was 16 feet square and 130 feet high. A smaller tower, 100 feet high, surmounted the main hall at the end. "The Grand Hotel is completed and handsomely furnished. It is much the largest and finest hotel in this region and, being situated on high ground, commands the most extended view of the lake."[11] With accommodations for 400 guests, the Grand Hotel had twice the capacity of the original Hotel Atheneum, which was completed a year later at Fair Point [Lanz 1999]. A photograph of the period reveals the massive proportions of this elaborate structure [Figure 11]. A second photograph affords a rare view of the richly furnished interior as it appeared in 1895 [Figure 12].

[11] *Jamestown Daily Herald*, June 29, 1880.

The substantial increase in the size of the hotel, and its relocation to a park area originally intended for the tents of families attending revival meetings, suggests the beginnings of a shift in purpose for Point Chautauqua. It is noteworthy that the open-air meeting place – called the "meeting ground" on Olmsted's plan and "the Pavilion" on the Association maps –, which was to have been located in the Corinthian Grove (see attached print), was apparently never built. No mention of this has been found in any newspaper article of the period nor has any trace been found on the ground.

Its Baptist founders had initially conceived Point Chautauqua as a religious enterprise similar to Chautauqua Assembly, which had previously been established across the lake at Fair Point by the Methodists. From the outset, therefore, the two groups were in direct competition with each other. As the rivalry grew, Dr. John Vincent, the dynamic head of Chautauqua Assembly, invited the Baptist leaders to his camp for a conference to sort out their differences. What Dr. Vincent proposed was a division of responsibilities in which Point Chautauqua's religious activities would henceforth take place at Fair Point. Under his plan, Point Chautauqua would henceforth be a strictly residential community. Though the Baptists later denied having agreed to this arrangement, Dr. Vincent subsequently reported widely on a number of occasions that this had been the case. However that may be, the following season at Point Chautauqua attracted a disappointing number of participants, and its religious function effectively ended from that date [Point Chautauqua 1975; Lanz 1999].[12]

Confirming the abandonment of its religious mission, the Point Chautauqua Association in 1885 announced its intent to convert the resort from a Baptist meeting ground to a place for the pursuit of health and pleasure. Point Chautauqua's Hartson Tabernacle became a Temple of Music and summer the-

43

---

[12] Mindful of this rivalry between the two camps, in 1883 Dr. Vincent placed a rising young Baptist scholar, William Rainey Harper, in charge of Chautauqua's entire educational program, which had just received a charter as a degree-granting university. By this stratagem, Vincent sought to preempt any move by Point Chautauqua to secure the services of this dynamic Baptist for any such program of its own [Simpson, 1999, pp. 51-52]. William Rainey Harper later climaxed an illustrious academic career by becoming the first president of the University of Chicago.

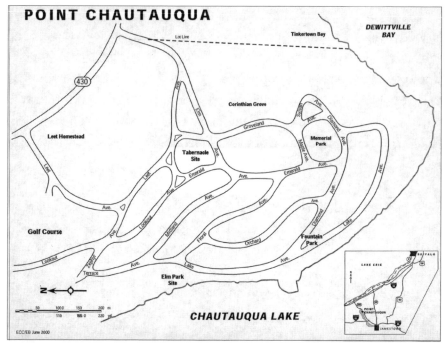

Figure 13 ❧ Present-day Point Chautauqua. A comparison of this map with Olmsted's planning map of 1875 (Figure 9) reveals significant similarities and differences. What remains remarkably unchanged after 125 years is the characteristically sinuous Olmsted road pattern. Notably missing are the large parks and other public spaces with which Olmsted had so generously provided the settlement. Absent, too, from the later map are the northern and southern extremities of the residential areas, which were planned but never constructed. Nevertheless, the modern residential sections of Point Chautauqua continue to occupy the same spaces as those of earlier times, and they still retain much of their original charm.

❧ Map by Emil Boasson, Computer Cartography Laboratory, Department of Geography, SUNY/Buffalo

ater. A roller-skating rink, bowling alley, and billiard room were added to the Tabernacle grounds. The division of labor between Point Chautauqua and its rival on the other side of the lake was thus complete: henceforth Dr. Vincent's Chautauqua was the center for religion and education; Point Chautauqua, the pleasure resort.

The expected customers for these new entertainment ventures failed to materialize in sufficient numbers, however, and Baptist operation of Point Chautauqua ended in bankruptcy in 1887. By court decree, the corporation "Point Chautauqua" was dissolved, with half of its 460 lots still unsold. The Grand Hotel, which apparently had never lacked for patrons, was nevertheless sold to private interests to settle the claims of the Association's bondholders. The great Tabernacle became derelict and was eventually razed in 1904. Properties still owned by the defunct Point Chautauqua Association – including the roadway system and unsold lots – were placed in the hands of a receiver. In the interest of preserving the community, Henry Clay Fry, a well-to-do Pittsburgh industrialist and one of the original Point Chautauqua property owners and a board member, eventually bought these holdings from the receiver. As a replacement for the Point Chautauqua Association, several leading residents formed a new organization, the Public Service Association, which assumed responsibility for the upkeep of public buildings, maintenance of the streets, and provision of lighting.

When the new Public Service Association assumed administrative control of Point Chautauqua, most, but not all, of the land appearing on Olmsted's original design had been developed. Some of the lots at the extreme north-western end had gone unsold, as well as several at the opposite end on the southeast. Hence the total space occupied by the community was somewhat smaller than initially intended, and this has not changed materially during the years since the Bible-camp era. A comparison of a current map of the community [Figure 13] with Olmsted's 1875 plan [Figure 9] reveals the portions of the original design that failed to materialize or that have been substantially altered.

The most conspicuously missing pieces today are the public lands with which Olmsted had so generously endowed the community, notably Ashmore Park, Elm Park, the Tabernacle site, and the Corinthian and Sylvan Groves. Nevertheless, it is easy to identify the spaces formerly occupied by these features because their locations and shapes are clearly defined by the well-preserved Olmsted road layout.

The contemporary map also fails to show the footpaths that lined each side of the roads in Olmsted's planning map. These are of special interest because they seem to be consistent with the Olmsted-Vaux principle of separating dif-

45

ferent kinds of traffic because of safety concerns – a concept that is much in evidence in their Central Park design. Whether these pathways were ever fully implemented at Point Chautauqua is unclear. The suggestion of such a path appears in an 1880s street scene on Floral Avenue [see Figure 14], and the remnants of an old concrete walk are still visible on one side of upper Diamond Avenue.

It is sometimes difficult to interpret Olmsted's exact intentions with respect to design details. As Charles Beveridge notes, "All his plans were in some sense preliminary, giving general indications of what was to occur on the land itself" [Beveridge 1999]. Nevertheless, the argument for the footpaths on the 1875 map rests on a solid foundation, being the logical expression of a firmly held design principle. On the other hand, given Olmsted's expressed reluctance to contribute designs for particular structures at Point Chautauqua, it seems that he was merely hinting at a logical allocation of land use with the trio of bathhouses that appear on The Strand in his map. This would be consistent with the Victorian-era cartographic practice of inserting symbolic figures on maps.

One intriguing feature of Olmsted's 1875 map is an apparent alternative entrance to the settlement, connecting with the northwestern end of Lookout Avenue. Though the map gives no indication where this presumed entrance was to lead, it seems likely that it would have been linked by a new road to the public highway at some point north of the upper Leet Avenue entrance. Charles Beveridge has proposed that Olmsted intended this never-constructed entrance to provide a direct link to the outside world for the residential sections of Point Chautauqua. It would thus have spared the people of this community from the rush of crowds entering Leet Avenue to attend religious events at the Tabernacle. Note that this northern sector of the 1875 map also shows two roads, Tybur and Highland Avenues, that were never constructed, not being required for this uncompleted portion of the original design. Nor were the three small parks planned for this end area ever built.

Although the residential portion of Point Chautauqua never fully reached the extreme ends of Olmsted's planning area, those portions that had been occupied by the 1890s have survived largely intact. The old houses, still in prime condition, offer well-preserved examples of Victorian-era architectural styles dating to the time of first settlement.

Nineteenth-Century Houses at Point Chautauqua

Indeed, one of the abiding legacies of Point Chautauqua's earliest period is its houses. Although the present housing stock as a whole varies in age and type, the community does appear to have a defining architectural form, represented by those house styles that date from the Baptist era – from the late 1870s to the early years of the twentieth century. Roughly a third of the present-day housing supply consists of these house types, which embody design features consistent with the romantic, picturesque spirit of Olmsted's landscape design as well as the Baptist religious ethic.

The record is not clear on the exact number of private dwellings constructed during the earliest period, and several, lost to fire or decay, have been replaced. Nevertheless, it appears that the majority of houses built during that age are still standing. Some 30 houses from the Baptist era (1870s and 1880s) remain today, and all of these are presently occupied. Another 20 or so existing houses were constructed in the 1890s and the early 1900s. Extensive alterations have obscured from view the early origins of several houses. Some are therefore older than they appear, because original architectural features have been removed or concealed under modern "improvements."

The original Point Chautauqua Association reserved for itself control over the style and character of all buildings erected on the grounds. It further imposed setback requirements for the buildings: 15-foot minimum for front yard; 5-foot minimum for side and rear yards. In keeping with its religious mission, the Association also covenanted that "no spiritous malt or intoxicating liquors or wine shall be sold or offered for sale or drank upon the premises hereby conveyed. That no barn, stable, shed or other place whatever, be erected or used for the keeping or stabling of dumb animals thereon." In addition, it reserved "the right and power . . . to control and direct as to all sanitary and health regulations upon the said premises" on penalty of forfeiture.[13] These restrictive covenants do not appear in deeds made since the collapse of the original Baptist-governed Point Chautauqua Association, but they emerge in all title searches.

It seems appropriate that the house types favored by Point Chautauqua's earliest residents were derived from that architectural movement known as the Gothic Revival. The original Gothic architecture appeared in France during the twelfth century and spread throughout Western Europe in the next four centuries. Among the defining features of this architecture were pointed arches, fine woodwork and stonework, and much use of ornamentation. The writer John Ruskin was one of those who urged a return to these earlier forms, arguing that the quality of medieval craftsmanship grew out of the morally superior culture of medieval times. The Gothic Revival encouraged freedom and honesty of design and construction, qualities that would have appealed to the religious community at Point Chautauqua.

The popularity of such forms here, as in other parts of the country during the period, was influenced by the publications of Andrew Jackson Downing, whose house-pattern books promoted this type of construction. Downing created the American cottage, a versatile design of Queen Anne derivation, that could be made grand or modest according to the owner's circumstances. Because of the ease with which any good carpenter could follow Downing's plans, this style (in its several variations) is commonly termed "carpenter Gothic," or "stick Gothic" for its lavish use of short pieces of wood to create decorative features. The origins of these house types so prevalent in Point Chautauqua's beginning years are of particular interest because of the relation-ship that had existed between Downing and Frederick Law Olmsted.[14]

48

---

[13] Warranty deed to Lot No. 446, dated April 15, 1882.

[14] It should be noted, however, that Olmsted did not offer explicit instructions regarding the style of housing at Point Chautauqua.

Point Chautauqua's earliest inhabitants displayed a notable preference for the stick style, which seems to have expressed the special qualities valued by a Baptist society:

> The Stick style of architecture is a direct outgrowth of Andrew Jackson Downing's theories of "truthfulness" in construction and the cultivation of "character," so important to Victorian society. Drawing its inspiration from the Gothic Revival simplicity, it was a distinctly American Style, developed by American technical ingenuity and designed for the growing working class. The style was a product of pattern-book architects, such as George Woodward. They were interested in producing inexpensive small houses for everyone, using wood of which there was an abundance. Stick architecture expressed an honesty and simplicity that was thought to be an inherent trait of Americans.[15]

Perhaps the most distinctive feature of the stick-style cottages was the profuse use of Gothic-inspired decorations: spires, turrets, arches, and elaborate ornamentation, adapted to the materials and woodworking tools of that age, especially the scroll saw.

The stick-Gothic form survives in many of Point Chautauqua's present-day houses, but few of these still retain the decorative details seen in old pictures from the Baptist era. Later generations removed most of these ornaments as they deteriorated in Western New York's severe winter climate, and have never replaced them because of maintenance cost. A few stick-style decorations have survived here and there, and some residents have begun to replace them. These later replicas, however, are not as elaborate as the originals. Only a few of the two-story porches remain, though in several cases these, too, are being restored.

---

[15] "Stick Style (1870-1880)," *Nineteenth Century Architecture in Geneva*. Geneva, New York, 1978.

Figure 14 ❧ Stick-Gothic houses on Floral Avenue in the 1880s. All the houses visible in this early print are still standing. The two nearest buildings have been considerably altered in appearance, but those in the background continue remarkably intact except for the loss of their original elaborate ornamentation.

❧ From *Souvenir of Lake Chautauqua* [New York: Adolph Wittemann, 1885]

Still remaining on Floral Avenue is a concentration of carpenter-Gothic houses, some of which were pictured in an 1880s souvenir book [Figure 14]. Over the years these have been substantially modified; no longer do they display the rich ornamentation seen in this old print. Others of this style are scattered along Lake, Lookout, and Leet Avenues. The old boardinghouses still in existence – now converted to private dwellings, except for Finn's Inn – were originally of a similar wood-frame construction. Large structures of this type are prominent in the middle section of Orchard Avenue.

Figure 15 ❧ Stick-style cottage at Floral and Emerald Avenues as it appeared in the 1880s. The present residents have undertaken a meticulous renovation of this unusually well-preserved example of Victorian-era construction. To ensure the authenticity of the restoration, the owners have enlarged detailed portions of old photographs to use as a guide in fashioning replacements for original architectural features.

❧ Historic photograph courtesy of Jerry and Gladys Loth

A prime example of stick-style architecture from Point Chautauqua's Baptist era stands today at the intersection of Emerald and Floral Avenues. In the 1880s this belonged to the Cadwell family, some of whom appear in the photo above [Figure 15]. The present owners have restored it to its original state, using old photographs as a guide. The house is $2^1/_2$ stories high, shaped in the form of a cross, and constructed of wood with clapboard siding. The portion of the house seen in the photo is the top of the cross; the base stem of the cross is concealed from view. As the photo shows, the steeply sloping roof originally had decorative crestings (probably cast iron) crowning the ridges. Extending on each side of the upper end of the cross are two-story porches supported by posts, which in earlier times were topped by elaborate decorations.

Figure 16 ❧ Contemporary photograph of a majestic nineteenth-century house at 6120 Floral. This stately dwelling, said to have belonged to one of the early Baptist preachers, looks out upon Lake Chautauqua from a commanding position on a steep slope rising above Elm Park. For most of its 120-some years it remained in the same family, who preserved much of its distinctive original character. Its current owner has scrupulously repaired and thoughtfully redecorated this old structure, adding Victorian-era ornamentation.   ❧ Photograph courtesy of Diana Holt

An imposing house farther down Floral Avenue, near its intersection with Lake, illustrates the creativity that was possible in carpenter-Gothic architecture. Originally the home of one of Point Chautauqua's first preachers, this structure remains little changed in general outline from earliest times. Although the elaborate stick-style ornamentation of the 1880s is gone, it retains the upper-level porches favored by the community's first residents. Among its interesting interior features is a winding staircase that climbs steeply through all $3^1/_2$ floors, ending in a large attic room offering magnificent vistas through dormers that face in all four directions. In their careful renovation of this old cottage, the present owners have striven to preserve its original character, as a recent photograph shows [Figure 16].

The steep terrain presented Point Chautauqua's early original builders with
unusual opportunities to exploit the possibilities of carpenter-Gothic style. An excellent example of this is a dwelling on the downhill side of Floral Avenue [Figure 17]. Because the elevation drops abruptly from the front of the building to the back, what appears as a conventional $2^1/_2$-story house on the street side proves to be a full $3^1/_2$-story house on the rear, offering splendid views of the lake from all three levels. This strategy was popular among Point

Figure 17 ❧ Resourceful adaptation to Point Chautauqua's sloping terrain: house at 6095 Floral. As in the case of the dwelling shown in the previous figure, the builders made creative use of the steep topography to create a uniquely functional design. At the lower elevation seen here, the rear of the house stands $3\frac{1}{2}$ stories high, and the favorable contour of the land permits full use of the light and airy ground floor as living quarters. From the rear, every floor provides an excellent view of Lake Chautauqua. The front of the house, at a substantially higher elevation, is entered from Floral Avenue at the second-floor level. The dwelling has a spacious setting, comprising eight of the original Olmsted lots, including a large area that once held a hotel complex known as the Barnes House (see Figure 26). ❧ Photograph courtesy of Diana Holt

Chautauqua's early settlers, who employed it in a variety of ways to gain maximum benefit from their scenic surroundings. After many years of neglect, this house had become structurally unsound by the late 1970s. At that point a new owner undertook extensive renovation of the building, shoring it up with a substantial masonry foundation and a completely reconstructed ground floor.

Standing side by side near the southern end of Lake Avenue are two distinctive Victorian-era houses that represent another adaptation of the carpenter-Gothic form (seen in a contemporary photograph [Figure 18, p. 54]). Unlike other Point Chautauqua cottages from the period, the house on the left features a prominent arched façade reminiscent of medieval Gothic times. This charming house appears in the turn-of-the-century picture [Figure 19, p. 55]. (Note the Grand Hotel in the background.) This exquisite old dwelling

53
❧

Figure 18 ❧ Distinctive variations on the carpenter-Gothic design: contemporary photo of two well-preserved dwellings on lower Lake Avenue. The quaint cottage on the left differs particularly from most of the other Victorian-era houses at Point Chautauqua in its prominent use of the arch, a Gothic Revival feature that was much in favor at the time. Both dwellings are scrupulously maintained and in excellent condition. They occupy one of the choicest stretches of waterfront land in the community, with unsurpassed views of the entire upper lake basin.

❧ Photograph courtesy of Diana Holt

remains in an excellent state of preservation, little changed after 120-some years of continual use.

An early cottage of a quite different type stands near the northern end of Lake Avenue [Figure 20]. By contrast with the elaborately ornamented carpenter-Gothic houses that predominated during the Baptist era, this tiny $1\frac{1}{2}$-story building has the narrow construction, steeply sloping roof, and simple ornamentation that characterized the wooden "tents" found in nineteenth-century Bible camps.[16] Looking out between two majestic European larch trees, this quaint survival from the Sunday-school camp era enjoys a commanding view of the upper basin of the lake. The only other existing examples of this architectural type at Point Chautauqua are a pair of tent houses on the waterfront at the intersection of Diamond and Lake Avenues. The two remain side by side, having been joined together with a middle section at some earlier time. They have been beautifully restored and fitted with decorative pieces reminiscent of carpenter-Gothic ornamentation.

---

[16] See Ellen Weiss, *City in the Woods: The Life and Design of an American Camp Meeting on Martha's Vineyard.* New York: Oxford University Press, 1987.

Figure 19 ❧ One of the carpenter-Gothic houses in Figure 18 as it appeared in 1900. The ghostly structure in the background is the Grand Hotel, which went up in flames two years after this picture was taken. This cottage was occupied for many generations by the pioneering family that built it, and later it served for a time as the home of Point Chautauqua's postmaster. ❧ Photograph courtesy of Helen Campbell

The restoration of 125-year-old houses presents practical difficulties, particularly of a structural nature. One of the most common structural weaknesses results from the nineteenth-century practice of using simple unmortared flagstone foundations to support dwellings intended in those days as mere summer cottages. In time these poorly supported structures have tended to weaken with the shifting of underlying strata and the effects of soil creep on steep slopes. The humid climate has also caused supporting timbers to rot away. Over the years, most owners have replaced these primitive foundations with concrete or masonry. Unfortunately, some neglected their properties until they deteriorated beyond salvaging. Often these buildings were allowed to decay as later generations found them inconvenient or outgrew them. In the past some of these cottages became derelict and were abandoned; often they were replaced with modern structures. The exquisite house shown in Figure

55
❧

Figure 20 ❧ Contemporary photo of rare Bible-camp-era "tent house" overlooking the lake from the northern end of Orchard Avenue. In Point Chautauqua's earliest years many of those who attended the revival meetings pitched tents on the small lots Olmsted had provided for this purpose. In time some of them chose to improve upon this spartan way of life by replacing the canvas tents with wooden structures of much the same form. This charming $1\frac{1}{2}$-story tent house has recently been lovingly restored by a new owner. Looking out upon Lake Chautauqua through two towering European larch trees, he is rewarded with one of the grandest vistas to be found anywhere along the waterfront.   ❧ Photograph courtesy of Diana Holt

21 is one that has escaped such an end, having recently been resurrected with loving care by new owners.

An historic cottage that has entirely lost its distinctive nineteenth-century features poses challenging restoration problems, but it can also present tempting opportunities. Generally, over many years, such a building will have

Figure 21 ❧ "Tottering" – a restored dwelling at 5497 Emerald Avenue. Despite the widely admired carpenter-Gothic lines of this quaint old house, it lay empty for many years following the death of its last occupant, growing increasingly dilapidated as time passed. Wholly neglected, the structure eventually fell into such disrepair that it began to list badly, leading neighbors to refer to it fondly as "Tottering." New owners have now restored the building to soundness and have imaginatively altered it in ways that have made it more livable. They have strengthened the building by providing it with a full basement and have replaced the decayed stick-Gothic ornamentation, relying upon period photographs to create precise duplicates of the original. Because the old Tottering was inconveniently small, they added a rear wing designed to replicate closely the main features of the older front section.

❧ Photograph courtesy of Diana Holt

passed through many hands, each new set of occupants altering it to their liking: adding wings, removing or enclosing porches, or stripping off ornamentation. In the end, the building has been so modernized that it no longer bears any resemblance to the charming carpenter-Gothic original. If, in time, new owners wish to restore the Victorian-era dwelling, they may find that no pictorial record remains to guide them. Faced with this quandary, some Point Chautauqua residents have effectively drawn upon their imaginations to re-create the past. An effective example of this appears in Figure 22.

Much of the nineteenth-century flavor of Victorian Point Chautauqua thus endures in its housing stock. The quiet, almost tranquil atmosphere of this residential community in the present era offers no suggestion of the boisterous summer resort that Point Chautauqua became following its brief time as a Bible

Figure 22 ❧ Imaginatively recreated Victorian-era cottage at 6037 Orchard. Reputed to be one of the oldest dwellings at Point Chautauqua, it was originally the home of Reverend Pease, owner of Pease Cottages, later renamed Bonnieview Lodge, which once stood next door (see Figure 25). New owners have thoroughly renovated and modernized this quaint dwelling. Newly constructed two-story open porches, fitted with specially designed ornamental railings, wrap around three sides of the building, offering a sweeping view of the upper basin of the lake. These porches replace a previous set that had been enclosed at an earlier time. ❧ Photograph courtesy of Diana Holt

camp, the period in which these oldest houses were built. Now, at the turn of the twenty-first century, it is hard to imagine that this was once a bustling community of hotels, inns, boardinghouses, shops, and a variety of other commercial establishments. Nearly every trace of that era has vanished. Point Chautauqua as a pleasure resort survives only in the memories of the oldest citizens.

C H A P T E R ❊ F O U R
Pleasure Resort

Figure 23 ❧   The Point Chautauqua waterfront about 1900. In this rare photograph the steamer *Aliquippa* is approaching the Point Chautauqua landing, where it will discharge its cargo. Its passengers and freight had been taken aboard at Mayville, having previously arrived by railway at the waterfront station in Mayville, the northern terminus on the lake. The *Aliquippa* will then likely proceed to Chautauqua Institution and other points on the route to its southern terminal at Jamestown. Several of the many hotels, inns, and boardinghouses that catered to Point Chautauqua's multitude of summer visitors are visible in this picture. The Grand Hotel, soon to be destroyed by a sensational fire, towers over the waterfront at the far right. High on the horizon, the Hartson Tabernacle, its majestic tower long since collapsed, forlornly looks down upon the scene, a reproachful reminder of Point Chautauqua's religious past. By 1904 it had been dismantled.   ❧ Courtesy of the Fenton Historical Society

y the end of the 1880s Point Chautauqua had abandoned its religious mission, but for many years afterward it continued to flourish and grow as a summer village and pleasure resort. A news account of 1900 reported that "Point Chautauqua today is one of the most prosperous resorts on the lake. Point Chautauqua is, however, a summer resort pure and simple. The religious meetings and schools the founders hoped to organize are things of the past."[17]   A turn-of-the-century photograph reveals a bustling Point Chautauqua waterfront dominated by hotels and other commercial structures and linked by a fleet of lake steamers to railway termi-

59
❊

[17]   *Jamestown Daily Herald*, August 14, 1900.

Figure 24 ❧ The Breeze Hotel, 1895. At the turn of the century, passengers disembarking lake steamers came immediately upon the Breeze Hotel. This formed the rear portion of a larger structure fronting on Lake Avenue, which contained a variety of commercial establishments. As seen in subsequent illustrations, this waterfront complex grew in size during the following century, continually adding new functions. Visible in the background of this photo is a portion of the seemingly ubiquitous Grand Hotel.   ❧ Courtesy of the Fenton Historical Society

nals at either end of the lake [Figure 23]. A closer view shows the Breeze Hotel, the first establishment that, in early years, greeted new arrivals as they disembarked [Figure 24].

THE HOTEL ERA

*F*or another half century – up until the Second World War – each new summer brought crowds of vacationers to Point Chautauqua. On the whole, the hotels, boardinghouses, and shops thrived. However, competition was intense; over the years a number of these enterprises failed – on occasion, dramatically.

Top: Figure 25 ❧ Bonnieview Lodge. Originally known as Pease's Cottages after the first owner, Reverend Pease, the Bonnieview commanded a superb site at the northern end of Lake Avenue. Behind the main building shown here were two smaller structures rented separately to visitors (see Figure 37). One of the oldest hostelries in the community, it continued to take in guests through the 1940s and remained a favorite dining spot for local residents, many of whom ate here nightly throughout the week. It had begun to deteriorate noticeably during the Second World War, however, and it was finally dismantled in the 1960s. Those who remember the magnificent vista from the upper porch, partially concealed by foliage in this photograph, declare the Bonnieview to have been fittingly named.   ❧ From the postcard collection of Ertem Beckman

Bottom: Figure 26 ❧ The Barnes House. This small inn, consisting of three adjacent buildings, occupied a site on the downhill side of Floral Avenue, directly across from the carpenter-Gothic houses shown in Figure 14. This establishment was destroyed by fire during the period between the World Wars.
                                     ❧ From the postcard collection of Ertem Beckman

61
❧

Top: *Figure 27* ❧ An early view of the Lake Side House. Later called the Lakeside Hotel, this popular establishment was strategically located on lower Diamond Avenue, close to the dock house and boat landing. As its name suggests, the Lakeside offered an incomparable view of the entire upper lake basin, as seen from the Lake Avenue side of the building. This hotel remained in operation for many years and is well remembered by longtime residents. Finally, with World War II approaching and the community in decline, it was torn down in or about 1940. ❧ Courtesy of the Fenton Historical Society

Bottom: *Figure 28* ❧ The Inn in earlier years. Occupying a site at the intersections of three of the most-traveled streets, Emerald, Diamond, and Orchard Avenues, this was the most centrally located and accessible of Point Chautauqua's commercial enterprises. Viewed here from its lower, Orchard Avenue, side, The Inn was the longest-lived and, in later years, the most popular of the larger hostelries at Point Chautauqua. ❧ From the postcard collection of Ertem Beckman

The Great Fire

Under private ownership, the Grand Hotel remained a popular attraction for a time, but it was never able to generate enough revenue to support its high-cost operation. The end came with spectacular suddenness:

> The Grand Hotel at Point Chautauqua was burned to the ground this morning [October 17, 1902]...The flames spread with amazing rapidity to every part of the building, and inside of three hours from the time the fire was discovered the magnificent structure was in ashes. There was not even a charred timber left on the site. . . . It was impossible to save anything from the burning building. The magnificent black walnut furniture with which the house was filled, the high-priced carpets, the costly china and silverware were consumed like so much straw. Not a single dollar's worth of goods was removed.[18]

The fire was proved to have been arson, and one of the owners was subsequently convicted of hiring the blaze set.

Loss of the Grand Hotel may have deprived Point Chautauqua of its most impressive architectural feature, but it did not leave the resort without accommodations for summer visitors. As early as 1884 the resort had acquired the Kinnear House and Pease's Cottages (later Bonnieview Lodge) on Lake Avenue [Figure 25], Thayer Cottage on Orchard, Barnes Cottages on Floral [Figure 26], Lake View and Clover Cottages on Midland, and Derby Cottage on Leet near the Tabernacle. These lesser establishments, large wooden-frame structures offering a dozen or more rooms each, continued to multiply throughout this period. By the beginning of the new century, they were joined by such larger inns and hotels as the Lake Side, on Diamond Avenue [Figure 27], and The Inn, at Diamond and Emerald [Figure 28].

63

---

18 *Jamestown Evening Journal,* October 17, 1902.

Top: Figure 29 ✺ The dock building and bowling alley as seen from the upper side, on Lake Avenue. The nearest approximation of a central business district at Point Chautauqua grew up around the boat landing, at the intersection of Lake and Diamond Avenues and across from Olmsted's Fountain Park (from which this photo was taken). On the right is the dock building, the top floor of which contained guest rooms and spaces for other purposes. The lower floors provided space for an ever-changing variety of business enterprises. At different times these included the community post office, an ice cream parlor, a gift shop, and a hairdresser. When the electric traction line reached the community in 1914, this building also housed the trolley station. At street level, the structure on the left contained the bowling alley.   ✺ Photograph courtesy of Helen Campbell

Bottom: Figure 30 ✺ The dock building and bowling alley viewed from below. The dock building appears more impressive when seen from the lakeshore side, which reveals its full three-story height. Judging by the vintage of the motor car parked above on Lake Avenue, this photograph seems to have been taken in the early 1920s. Later the dock building acquired an addition, which was attached on the left side as viewed here. The new wing was used as a dance hall and for performances by the touring theatrical troupe that came to Point Chautauqua each summer, as well as for other community events. A boat-rental service occupied the lower floor of the bowling alley, seen on the right in this photograph.   ✺ Photograph courtesy of Helen Campbell

As the pace of activity at Point Chautauqua accelerated, a business center grew up around the boat landing. The main focus was the dock building, which was enlarged over the years and came to house a variety of establishments [Figures 29 and 30]. Above were rooms for guests, and below were shops of different kinds: a post office, an ice cream parlor, a gift shop, a hair dresser, and, by 1914, a trolley station. The building next door, on the south, housed a bowling alley at street level and a boat livery (boat-rental service) below, at water level. A community swimming area adjacent to the boat livery featured a water slide, an attraction much favored by the young.

Travel to Point Chautauqua from Pittsburgh and Cleveland, and from Buffalo and points east, was by rail to Mayville, Westfield, or Jamestown. The map [Figure 31] shows the rail lines serving the Lake Chautauqua region at the turn of the century. At Mayville or Jamestown, visitors transferred to large, double-deck steamboats, which provided service to all major points around the lake. Some of these plied a triangular route between Mayville's waterfront train station and Point Chautauqua and Chautauqua Institution. Steamboats continued to be the chief mode of local travel until the early 1920s, when they lost out to competition from the electric trolley.

Turn-of-the-Century Housing

Houses built during the 1890s and early 1900s continued to reveal a preference for large $2^1/_2$-story wood frame construction of the Queen Anne style, following in the tradition established in the community's earliest years. The dwellings that remain from this era can be distinguished from the Gothic Revival houses of earlier times by their roof lines, which are not as steeply pitched.

Early in the twentieth century, another house type became popular at Point Chautauqua: this was the Craftsman style, associated with Gustav Stickley of Syracuse, New York, editor of the *Craftsman* magazine. Like the earlier stick design, the Craftsman style appears to have been well suited to the traditional values of the community. Stickley declared his houses to be "based on the big

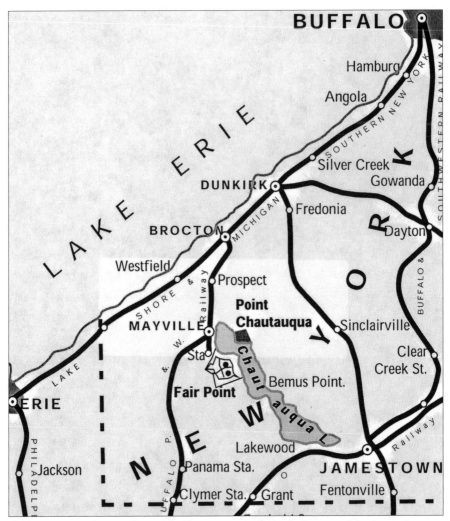

Figure 31 ❧ A map of steam railways in the Chautauqua region during the latter part of the nineteenth century. From the outset Lake Chautauqua was well served by a network of railways providing good connections for summer visitors from Pittsburgh, Buffalo, Cleveland, and points beyond. Much consolidation of railway systems took place throughout this period, and the names of the lines on this map underwent many changes over the years.

❧ Map by Emil Boasson, Computer Cartography Laboratory, Department of Geography, SUNY/Buffalo

❧

fundamental principles of honesty, simplicity, and usefulness – the kind of houses that children will rejoice all their lives to remember as 'home,' and that give a sense of peace and comfort to the tired men who go back to them when the day's work is done."[19] Contributing to the nationwide popularity of Craftsman

---

[19] Quoted in Russell Lynes, *The Tastemakers*. New York, 1949, p. 188.

Top: Figure 32 ❧ Craftsman-style house at 6007 Diamond Avenue. Point Chautauqua has several houses of this comfortable and durable design, which enjoyed national popularity in the 1920s. This style takes its name from the *Craftsman* magazine, the early twentieth-century publication that introduced it to the public. The widespread acceptance of Craftsman-style houses was due in large measure to their ready availability from mail-order firms, which shipped them to customers in kit form. Contractors engaged in later years to remodel Craftsman houses at Point Chautauqua have been impressed by their remarkable sturdiness, which results from the cantilever design of their primary structural members. ❧ Photograph courtesy of Diana Holt

Bottom: Figure 33 ❧ Colonial Revival house at 6118 Midland Avenue. Overlooking the Tabernacle grounds, this house was constructed in 1913 of bricks said to have been imported by the owner from his ancestral Germany. Quite large by Point Chautauqua standards, it contains ten bedrooms and has fireplaces on both the first and second floors. It was the first dwelling in the community to be wholly self-contained, with hot and cold running water, gas-fired central heating, and its own electric-generating system. ❧ Photograph courtesy of Diana Holt

houses during that era was their availability through mail-order houses, which shipped them in kit form to their destinations.

At Point Chautauqua, most of the dwellings of this kind are $1^1/_2$ stories high and have moderately sloping roofs. This is the most common house type on Diamond Avenue, leading down to the waterfront, and a few appear at other locations throughout the community. Altogether, Point Chautauqua has a dozen or so of these unusually sturdy houses [see Figure 32].

An interesting anomaly dating to this period is a large yellow brick structure at the intersection of Lookout and Emerald Avenues, overlooking the Tabernacle grounds. Using bricks said to have been imported from his ancestral Germany, a prosperous Pittsburgh distiller built this elaborate (by Point Chautauqua standards) establishment in 1913. It is in the Colonial Revival style [Figure 33].

Most of the older dwellings were intended for summer use only, and, though of fair size and durable construction, they generally lacked lath-and-plaster interiors. Nearly all have since been modernized, and several have been winterized. This is particularly true of those belonging to the community's growing number of year-round residents, who now number more than 20 families. However, many of the old dwellings that remain unoccupied in the winter still have unplastered walls, often covered with wainscoting or wood paneling.

BETWEEN THE WARS

When the First World War came to an end, the people of Point Chautauqua, of course, could not have anticipated the profound changes that the next two decades would bring. The inter-war period was destined to produce major advances in technology, fundamental social change, and catastrophic economic and political events. Though its summer residents and visitors were bent on the pursuit of relaxation and pleasure, this resort community was not to escape the effects of affairs in the outside world. For Point Chautauqua this was to be a time of transition, which would leave the community altogether transformed in its function and social makeup.

Turning Point

As the twenties got under way, the community paused to look back at its first half century. At a convocation on the evening of August 22, 1926, Point Chautauqua celebrated its fiftieth anniversary with reminiscences by community leaders who had been present during the early days. Reverend H. M. Tenney reflected on the creation of the settlement – the Baptist land purchase from the Leet brothers, the engaging of Frederick Law Olmsted to lay out the roads, lots, and public areas. He then paid tribute to those who were instrumental in preserving the community during its times of financial distress. Chief among these early patrons, and a director of the original Point Chautauqua Association, was Henry C. Fry, who was present at the celebration and shared his own recollections with the group.

Across the years, innovations in transportation have continued to affect Point Chautauqua in many ways, just as they have in the country at large. During the nineteenth century and well into the twentieth, local roads were exceedingly primitive [Figure 34]. The community was therefore forced to rely largely upon lake steamers for the movement of people and supplies. Thus, for many years a coal dock was a necessary feature at the southern end of the waterfront. On the eve of the First World War, however, a succession of new

Figure 34 ❧ The main entrance to Point Chautauqua as it looked in earlier years. The primitive state of both public and private roads before the middle of the twentieth century is apparent from this photograph showing the intersection of Leet Avenue with the highway connecting to the outside world (now State Route 430). However, the community enjoyed convenient and relatively quick access to other destinations via regular steamer service on Lake Chautauqua, with its links to a well-developed regional and national rail system. Note the palmist's sign.
❧ Photograph courtesy of Helen Campbell

forms of transportation began to appear. The first of these was the electric trolley.

Trolley service came first to Jamestown in 1891; eventually two of these light-rail lines extended along both sides of the lake to Mayville and then on to Westfield. The company serving the Point Chautauqua side of the lake was the Jamestown, Westfield and Northwestern; on the western side, it was the Chautauqua Traction Company. At Westfield, passengers could transfer to other electric interurban lines providing service to Cleveland and Buffalo, or to conventional steam railways that stopped at that same point (see map of transport connections in the 1920s [Figure 35]).[20]

70

20 Comparing this map with the transport map of the 1880s (above) discloses not only the addition of electric traction lines but also a number of changes in the conventional steam railway system since the earlier period.

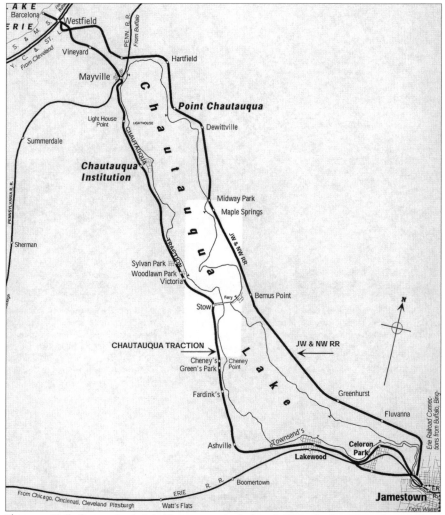

Figure 35 ❧ Trolley lines serving the Lake Chautauqua region in the early 1900s. An electric interurban railway ran down each side of the lake, providing quick transportation for communities previously dependent upon leisurely steamboat travel. Point Chautauqua's summer population was able to fashion a new lifestyle around this convenient service. Wives and children would spend the entire summer at Point Chautauqua, while husbands were able to work at their city jobs during the week and commute by a combination of electric interurban and steam railways to rejoin their families at the lake on weekends. By the end of World War II these light-rail electric lines were gone, supplanted by the automobile.

❧ Map by Emil Boasson, Computer Cartography Laboratory, Department of Geography, SUNY/Buffalo. Adapted from map in *Trolleys of Jamestown and Chautauqua Lake*, by Helen Ebersole, published for the Fenton Historical Society by the Chautauqua Regional Press of Westfield (New York), 1998. Used with permission of the Fenton Historical Society.

❧

Figure 36 ❧ Trolley stop at Point Chautauqua as seen from the back of a rail car. By the 1940s both Point Chautauqua and the trolley line had fallen upon hard times. This view from the rear window of a southbound car reveals a dock building grown rather shabby and the area around it unkempt. Still, even at this late date, the trolley provided a convenient way for Point Chautauquans to shop in neighboring towns and for their children to visit the amusement park at Midway. During the off-season, children of families wintering at Point Chautauqua rode the trolley to high school in Mayville. ❧ Courtesy of the Fenton Historical Society

By 1914 electric traction service had reached Point Chautauqua, where the tracks skirted the shoreward side of Lake Avenue, with a passenger stop at the boat dock [Figure 36]. Point Chautauquans found the trolleys very grand, with their corduroy seats and rear observation platforms. They also found their ways of life greatly changed by the availability of high-speed rail service providing quick, convenient connections with other communities around the lake and superior access to the world beyond. Residents could shop in Mayville or Jamestown, children could visit the amusement park at Midway, and husbands could commute on weekends from their jobs in St. Louis, Pittsburgh, or Buffalo. Much as the electric trolleys were appreciated in the early days, they were to have a limited life span. Auto travel was already beginning to encroach upon the long-held monopoly of the established modes of public transportation, and by the 1930s the motor car was gaining ascendancy. The electric traction service managed somehow to survive through the inter-war

Figure 37 ❧ Point Chautauqua waterfront in the 1940s, as seen from the air. Though the electric interurban was nearing the end of its line by this date, the trolley tracks and overhead system of electric wires still occupied much of The Strand. This unusual view reveals the dock building (beneath the aircraft wing) after the addition of its north annex, which housed the dance hall. Here, too, the summer theatrical troupe performed. The dwelling directly across Lake Avenue from the dock building served as the post office in some years. Beyond it is a stately carpenter-Gothic house dating to the founding days of the community; recently it was torn down and replaced with a duplex. In the middle distance stands the Bonnieview Lodge, with its two outlying rental cottages and the home of its owner (see Figures 22 and 25, pp. 58 and 61). ❧ Courtesy of the McClurg Museum

era [Figure 37], but soon after the end of the Second World War the trolleys followed the steamboat service into extinction.

Life in a Summer Resort

During the inter-war era, community organization at Point Chautauqua underwent considerable change. The community's main benefactor, Mr. Fry, died in 1929, leaving the balance of his Point Chautauqua holdings to his five children. A number of community leaders thereupon incorporated a Point Chautauqua Land Company, to which Fry's heirs deeded over their interests in Point Chautauqua "in consideration of $1.00 and more."[21] The Land Com-

73

---

[21] Leet 1957, p. 4

pany assumed responsibility for supplying such community services as water supply and maintenance of roads, public lands, and waterfront facilities. It also bought and operated the golf course adjoining the settlement on the north.

Other organizations also came into being to provide for the social needs of a very active summer community. One of these was the Point Chautauqua Club, which maintained a meeting hall used for entertainments and Sunday services throughout the season. Another was the Ladies' Auxiliary, which supplied a club room, ran the Sunday evening song service and the Sabbath school, and organized social activities on weekdays.

Though the founders of the first Point Chautauqua Association had been persons of considerable financial means, the early members of the original religious colony at the Point were fairly representative of the socioeconomic spectrum that constituted Baptist Church membership. Secularization of the community, however, brought changes in the makeup of the summer population and produced a new social structure that was to prevail until World War II. It was the Pittsburgh industrialist Henry C. Fry who had rescued Point Chautauqua from receivership, and it was a group of well-to-do Pittsburghers who supplied the majority of summer residents in subsequent years.

At the beginning of each summer the families would come with their servants and personal belongings and settle in for the season, either in their own cottages or in houses rented from local year-round residents. Pocketing ample rentals, the latter would vacate their homes for the period and live elsewhere until fall. Vacationing wives and children would remain at Point Chautauqua throughout the warm season, while husbands generally came only on weekends, arriving by overnight train on Saturday morning and leaving on Sunday night in order to be back for work in the city the next day. Point Chautauqua's social makeup thus underwent an annual seasonal change, with the arrival of a summer population largely comprising members of the leisure class, their servants, and those who operated and staffed the commercial establishments.

It has been reckoned that, throughout the 1920s and into the 1940s, the summer population included about 85 percent Pittsburghers, 10 percent Clevelanders, and 5 percent Buffalonians.[22] At the time, Point Chautauqua was looked upon as a prestigious resort where prominent citizens vacationed. At some point during the season, the society editor of one of the three Pittsburgh papers would spend a day or so at the Point taking pictures for a story on the Sunday society page.[23]

The summer population swelled greatly during those resort years as growing numbers came to stay at the many hotels and boardinghouses. Life centered upon water sports, dinner in the evening at the hotels, promenades along the waterfront, cocktail parties, and dancing to band music at The Inn. At dusk, streets were crowded with people strolling about in the warm evening air, chatting and exchanging greetings with passing friends and acquaintances. The summer-evening stroll remains a local custom today, though the number of walkers is much reduced.

The Inn became a focal point for social life in the community – a place to hold parties and wedding receptions as well as a spot to gather for evening entertainment [Figure 38]. The Inn periodically issued a broadside called *The Point* (known familiarly as the "Pink Sheet" for its color), which carried pictures and small news items about individuals and families of the community.

---

[22] In ascribing Point Chautauqua's inhabitants to particular cities, we follow the local practice of citing the metropolitan areas from which these families come, such as Greater Cleveland or Greater Pittsburgh. For example, when asked, individuals from suburban East Aurora or Hamburg will usually give Buffalo as their place of origin. The proportion of families coming from any given area has shifted over time. To some extent this relates to the quality of transport connections and the availability of alternative vacation opportunities in a given period. Thus, prior to the auto age, Pittsburghers found the trip to Lake Chautauqua particularly convenient because of the excellent rail connections from that city. In earlier times they could disembark at Mayville's lakefront train station and go directly to an adjacent dock. There they would board a lake steamer that would take them either to Point Chautauqua or to the Chautauqua Assembly grounds. By the turn of the century, the Pennsylvania Railroad's Pittsburgh-Buffalo line offered direct overnight service to nearby Westfield, where passengers could board an electric trolley that delivered them to the Point Chautauqua waterfront. The lack of large bodies of unpolluted freshwater in the highly industrialized Pittsburgh area also contributed to its disproportionately large representation at Point Chautauqua until recent times; Clevelanders and Buffalonians had other alternatives close at hand. A third explanation for the composition of Point Chautauqua's population is the common tendency for people to be influenced in their vacationing decisions by a desire to be with friends and relatives, thus creating "migration streams."

[23] Personal communication from Ford Cadwell, who was born at Point Chautauqua in 1904 and subsequently lived in nearby Dewittville. Mr. Cadwell's family were builders and were responsible for constructing ten of the houses at the Point.

Figure 38 ❧ Aerial photo of The Inn. Two events contributed to the surge in popularity enjoyed by The Inn in later years: One was a change of ownership about 1930 and the thorough renovation that followed. This view of the Emerald Avenue side from above clearly shows the additions built at that time. The second favorable event was the repeal of Prohibition. The new owner remodeled the lobby to accommodate a bar, which became so popular that it had to be supplemented with a rathskeller in the basement. To extend The Inn's service area beyond the community, the proprietor installed a boat dock (visible on the upper left), which attracted the nautical crowd from miles around. A good restaurant completed this successful combination, enabling The Inn to become the main social center of the community. In the 1950s, however, The Inn changed hands and soon thereafter failed because of mismanagement. Also appearing in this photograph is another, smaller establishment, the Greehald (later the Balaton Villa), visible on the upper right.   ❧ Courtesy of the McClurg Museum

The proprietor and his wife were unofficial host and hostess of most community events. They presided over the weekly baseball game, for which everyone invariably turned out. (The innkeeper was always the catcher.) They put on children's parties, they personally greeted all new guests and saw them off when they departed, and between times they circulated among the patrons of the ground-floor cocktail lounge.

During this period The Inn extended its influence well beyond the boundaries of this small resort community. A path, which still exists, led directly from The Inn to the lakeshore, where a landing pier stood ready to receive guests coming from around the lake in their own boats. Arriving patrons would tie up their craft and proceed to The Inn for cocktails and dinner. Every Thursday The Inn hosted the weekly meeting of the Kiwanis Club. In time the proprietor of The Inn bought the Point Chautauqua golf course, which had, and still has, region-wide clientele. The clubhouse, which stood near the intersection of Leet and Zephyr, became a secondary center of community social life – another place to hold parties and visit with friends.

The Great Depression, which caused such distress throughout the country during these times, at first had only a limited effect on Point Chautauqua. The summer people who came here were an affluent group on the whole, and many were able to maintain their customary pattern of life throughout the period. Not all were so fortunate, however, and the number of summer visitors began to dwindle as the national economy worsened. The approaching Second World War contributed further to the declining patronage at the inns and hotels. By the eve of U.S. entry into the war, new construction had virtually halted in the community, and many older houses were falling into disrepair.[24]

Perhaps fifteen to twenty of Point Chautauqua's existing houses belong to this period. This group offers a greater range of size than the buildings of previous eras. A few of the inter-war dwellings are of the Craftsman type, but several are of the Bungalow style, another Stickley-inspired design that came into favor in the 1920s. Their distinguishing features are low, horizontal lines, hipped or gabled roofs, and relatively plain exteriors. Usually a gable extends over the front porch.[25] Two $1^1/_2$-story bungalows are on lower Diamond Avenue overlooking Fountain Park, and two others are on Maple Avenue across from Memorial Field [Figure 39]. Also dating from this period are two small single-story cottages on Emerald Avenue, between Maple and Floral. Originally constructed by The Inn to serve as overflow facilities, these initially lacked kitchens. Subsequent owners, however, have neatly modernized them for use as summer cottages.

---

[24] See "100th Anniversary of Point Chautauqua Observed" in *Point Chautauqua Centennial Issue*, August 1975, p. 1.
[25] *Landmarks of Oswego County*, Syracuse University Press, 1988, p. 62.

Figure 39 ❧ Two bungalows on Maple Avenue. During the 1920s Point Chautauqua acquired several of these small $1^1/_2$-story houses with sloping roofs. The name "bungalow" is derived from a Hindi word meaning "house in the Bengali style," a reference to a popular architectural type borrowed from British India. With their high ceilings, large doors and windows, and shady eaves and verandas, bungalows make ideal summer cottages.

❧ Photograph courtesy of Diana Holt

Just below Memorial Field on upper Diamond Avenue is another distinctive product of this period – a substantial wood-frame building with a hip roof and surrounded by extensive grounds occupying a bluff with a commanding view of the lake. This house lies within the area that Olmsted had reserved for "The Hotel." Built shortly after World War I, this year-round residence has a number of bedrooms and a large downstairs living area heated by a big fireplace.

As the 1930s grew to a close, the stirring of events in the world beyond began to intrude upon the genteel way of life at Point Chautauqua. The accustomed daily routines of wives and children and maids continued as usual throughout the week and, as usual, husbands returned for weekends of boating, fishing, and Land Company meetings. Yet the sense of impending foreign wars – though seemingly still remote – introduced a vague note of apprehension. Younger men from the community enlisted in the military, relatives arrived from abroad after hazardous sea journeys, the number of customers at The Inn dwindled, and the quality of merchandise on store shelves deteriorated as war preparation began to absorb more of national production. The once-settled social climate at Point Chautauqua had been disturbed. The 1940s were to bring still more upheaval and change.

CHAPTER FIVE

Residential Community

DECLINE & RENEWAL

*W*hen World War II arrived at last with all its disruptions, the old way of life at Point Chautauqua effectively ended. Generational change also contributed to the transition. By the 1950s the number of prominent Pittsburghers spending their summers at Point Chautauqua had dwindled substantially. Many had grown old; some had died. Their children had scattered throughout the country and found it increasingly difficult to leave their homes and jobs to return to the Point. In many cases money and properties had been divided among several heirs, forcing the new-generation families to share family cottages with relatives, often an unsatisfactory arrangement. Nor did postwar families have the domestic help that had so eased the lives of their parents and grandparents. In time many children of the old families stopped coming to Point Chautauqua altogether.

Last of the Hotels

For a while longer The Inn remained a social center for Point Chautauqua and much of the Lake Chautauqua region. Eventually it, too, went into decline as its longtime proprietor grew old and retired. By the end of the 1950s The Inn had closed for good, leaving no comparable institution to perform its organizing role in the social life of the community. Soon thereafter this landmark of an era was torn down, leaving a large vacant space in the area it had once commanded.

During the Second World War and immediately afterward, much of Point Chautauqua's housing stock fell into decay and neglect, and several houses became vacant. From the 1940s through the 1960s only 10 new dwellings were constructed, some of these on the high bluff on Lookout Avenue downslope from the golf course. They are medium-size frame structures, averaging four bedrooms. Another house built immediately after the war is a rambling one-story, California-style house with stucco finish occupying the old swimming-pool area at the far south end of Lake Avenue on Olmsted's Strand.

As the postwar generation lost interest in maintaining the houses, property values deteriorated and the Land Company was forced to sell off some of its holdings. One of the first to go was the golf course, which was sold early on to the proprietor of The Inn. Other landholdings, including the Tabernacle site and the woods, were given over to creditors to settle debts. The cost of maintaining the roads became increasingly onerous, and in the late 1950s the community successfully prevailed upon the Town of Chautauqua to assume their ownership and upkeep. By the end of the decade Point Chautauqua had reached its lowest ebb. Several houses stood empty, and most could have been had for only a few thousand dollars.

Transformation

In the end, however, low property values proved to be a positive attraction for a particular group of newcomers. In the early 1950s Hungarian refugees living in Cleveland discovered Point Chautauqua's virtues as a site for holding rural retreats of the kind to which they had been accustomed in their native land. Enfolded within forest-covered hills, Lake Chautauqua offered a nostalgic appeal to Cleveland's Hungarian émigrés because of its resemblance to their native Lake Balaton. Having fled Hungary with few material possessions, they found Point Chautauqua's low property prices a special inducement. A further attraction was the community's quaint, mellowed, nineteenth-century charm.

During the 1960s the Hungarian population of Point Chautauqua swelled until, by the end of the decade, more than a dozen families held property in the

Figure 40 ❧ The Balaton Villa. Longtime residents recall this in earlier days as the Greehald, an upscale rooming house with several apartments. In the 1960s a family from Cleveland purchased the Greehald and converted it into an Hungarian inn and restaurant, which they renamed the Balaton, after the fondly remembered lake of that name in their native land. The Balaton Villa perished in a fire at Christmas 1975.

❧ From the postcard collection of Ertem Beckman

settlement. At one time, five Hungarian-operated hostelries, bearing such names as Balaton Villa [Figure 40], Halásztanya, and Loon Lodge, were bringing substantial numbers of Hungarians as summer visitors to the community. These enlivened the social atmosphere with their colorful festivals.

Meanwhile, some of the longtime residents had also taken steps to renew the community. In the mid-1960s they undertook a beautification program: clearing and trimming the public lands, planting and maintaining flower beds in the triangular plots at Olmsted's road intersections, and constructing tennis courts at Memorial Park, which occupies the lower portion of the area designated as Ashmore Park on the original Olmsted design. In 1967 the first of Point Chautauqua's community picnics was held [Point Chautauqua 1975, p. 1].

81

Thus, in the years following the Second World War, Point Chautauqua was transformed into a community altogether different from the pleasure resort of earlier times. Changed circumstances naturally called for a different kind of community governance. Ever since the demise of the original Point Chautauqua Association in 1887, the Public Service Association had looked after community affairs. To accommodate the new problems of the postwar era, this body reorganized in 1948, taking once again the historic title Point Chautauqua Association. Then, in 1957, the new Association filed with the State of New York for articles of incorporation.

This marked an important step in democratizing community affairs. In 1875 the founding body of that name had been a joint-stock company of fifteen Baptist ministers and lay members dedicated to furthering the church mission. Its successor, the Public Service Association, an elite group of leading property owners, had managed community affairs in a paternalistic manner. On the other hand, upon becoming a State-chartered corporation, the new Point Chautauqua Association was obliged by its charter to open its membership to all owners of property in the community. Under its bylaws, each household is entitled to vote on issues raised at the annual meetings. A board of governors, elected from the membership, oversees community matters throughout the year [Leet 1957; Point Chautauqua 1975].

The immediate incentive in 1957 for incorporating the Association was to solve the long-standing issue of maintaining the Olmsted-designed road system. Since the founding of the community, ownership of the roads had remained in the hands of adjacent property owners, which required a degree of coordination difficult to achieve among a disparate group of mostly summer residents. By incorporating, the Association was able to receive title to roads and rights of way, making it possible for the Town of Chautauqua to assume maintenance of the system. With its superior equipment, the town has substantially improved the quality of the roads in recent years and has kept them remarkably clear of winter snows for the growing number of year-round residents.

On July 12, 1975, the residents of Point Chautauqua assembled at the neighboring Dewittville fire hall to celebrate the one-hundredth anniversary of the founding of the original Point Chautauqua Association.[26] Several longtime residents were still on hand to share their collections of mementos from early days – photographs, copies of early newspapers, old postcards, and other remembrances. The following August members of the community assembled a commemorative newspaper called *Point Chautauqua: Centennial Issue*, which recorded the event and reprinted valuable news accounts from historic publications and documents.

THE LAST QUARTER-CENTURY

*S*ince its revival in the late 1960s, Point Chautauqua has enjoyed uninterrupted growth and prosperity. Many new homes have been built and old ones renovated, modernized, and enlarged. As appreciation for the charm and grace of Point Chautauqua's stock of Victorian-era houses has grown, several of these fine old structures have been returned to their earlier grandeur, their multi-story porches and decorative trim restored. Today the ninety-some homes at Point Chautauqua exhibit well-kept lawns and gardens. Nearly all of these are occupied by the families of their owners; only one or two strictly rental properties exist. The old hotels have vanished, and only one small inn remains, permitted to continue operating by a grandfather clause in the otherwise exclusively residential zoning regulations. Property values have risen steadily, and the demand for houses placed on the market is strongest in the Chautauqua region – a consequence of the comforting sylvan atmosphere created by Olmsted's natural setting [Point Chautauqua 1975, p. 1].

Housing Renewal

As, one by one, the hotels and inns disappeared, additional land became available for private housing. Many of the sites freed up by the departure of these commercial establishments were prime locations, having been chosen

---

[26] That such meetings have had to take place outside the settlement in recent times is a measure of Point Chautauqua's transformation from a pleasure resort abundantly provided with public facilities to a strictly residential community entirely lacking indoor accommodations for public assembly.

by hoteliers especially for their superb views and access to the waterfront. Thus the fourteen new houses constructed in the 1970s enjoy this locational advantage. Most were constructed by a local builder, who favored a Swiss chalet style of architecture. Small to medium in size, they average three bedrooms and are of wood construction.

Restoration and modernization of historic houses has continued from the 1980s to the present. Ten new houses have also been built, including a very large wooden structure of modern design located on the southern end of the waterfront. Two others – one a medium-size ranch-style and another of individual wood-frame construction – occupy a portion of the property where The Inn once stood. On the margin of Olmsted's Sylvan Grove, fronting on Groveland Avenue, is another newly constructed two-story frame house. This residence occupies the site of Henry C. Fry's dwelling, which had become derelict in recent times. Except for a split-level frame house on Emerald Avenue, the remaining new dwellings are medium-size, ranch-style houses.

One dwelling erected in this recent period is of special interest because it represents a return to the architecture of Point Chautauqua's earliest period. This new house, constructed in the traditional carpenter-Gothic style, is located on the entry road, Leet Avenue, where it intersects with Emerald Avenue, the main arterial leading into the heart of the community [Figure 41]. Appropriately, this re-creation of the settlement's traditional house type looks out upon the historic site of the old Hartson Tabernacle. The owner, an engineer by training, undertook a careful search of the literature on house styles of the Victorian era and, with the aid of an architect, produced a design that is consistent with the architectural tradition of Point Chautauqua.

84

The owner of this new Gothic-style dwelling, a year-round resident, used modern materials and construction techniques to replicate the traditional form. In this way he was able to create a structure that could comfortably withstand the severe winters of the Allegheny foothills. This house replaces one of the original carpenter-Gothic buildings of the Baptist era, which had long been

Figure 41 ⁂ Carpenter-Gothic residence of modern construction on Leet Avenue. Located directly across from the Tabernacle grounds, this graceful house discerningly preserves the charm of Point Chautauqua's earliest architectural style while benefiting from the latest materials and techniques of contemporary building methodology. It occupies the site of an 1880s structure that had fallen into ruin after lying empty and abandoned for many years.
⁂ Photograph courtesy of Diana Holt

abandoned following the death of its last occupant – a music teacher and opera singer – and had fallen into ruin. Before dismantling the remains of the old building, the present owner retrieved the surviving pieces of the original ornamentation, which he duplicated and added to the new structure. This example has demonstrated to the community the practicality of combining traditional architectural styles with modern standards of comfort and efficiency.

Population Change

Many properties have changed hands in the decades since Point Chautauqua's resurrection, and this has brought a gradual shift in the makeup of the population. Most of the Hungarian families have departed in recent years. Some of the original members of this group have died, while others, as they have aged, have found the long trip from Cleveland increasingly tiring. Moreover, as Hungarian families have prospered and become integrated into the general culture of the country, they have no longer had to depend upon summer outings for mutual reinforcement against homesickness in a new land. Many of the new generation have acquired other interests and have scattered widely through the country. This generational change among Point Chautauqua's Hungarian population mirrors the experience of old-time residents.

Only five Hungarian families remain today. In each case, the family has remained because of the abiding affection of its younger members for Point Chautauqua. The Hungarian inns and lodges have all gone. Arrival of the Hungarians at the Point in the late 1960s, when its fortunes were at their lowest, had helped revive property values and dissolve the pervasive atmosphere of decay in the 1950s. Their presence also lent a more cosmopolitan air to the community, and this has served to attract a more diverse population than that of earlier times.

Many of the newest property owners come from Cleveland; several are from Buffalo. A growing number of retirees have taken up permanent year-round residence at the Point, and several younger families with local employment make the Point their full-time home. Unlike the families of the industrialists who had been the dominant group during much of Point Chautauqua's first century, the latest comers pursue a variety of occupations.

Despite the influx of new people, however, several of the old families are still represented in the community, some occupying houses that have been in family hands for many generations. Indeed, there has been a resurgence of enthusiasm for Point Chautauqua among the grandchildren of the old families. Repeating the cycle of two generations earlier, many of these people are returning, despite disappointment in some cases that old homesteads no longer remain in the family. Though reduced in number from previous times, the latest members of these old-time families preserve an intense loyalty and affection for Point Chautauqua. The Point is the common denominator for these families. It is "home," and the annual Point picnic is a grand reunion with childhood friends.

The rising popularity of Point Chautauqua, both as a place to live and as a place to vacation, has therefore effectively erased the postwar perception of Point Chautauqua as a decaying relic of another age. Whereas the record shows only 65 families in residence at the settlement's nadir in the 1950s, today's list contains more than 90 names.

Community Life in the New Age

Social life at Point Chautauqua is quite different now than it was in the heyday of the Pittsburgh industrialists – that era when floods of summer visitors filled the many inns and boardinghouses. No longer do families don their formal evening attire for dinner and dancing at The Inn. Yet the traditional evening stroll still persists, as does the partying among families and friends. As in earlier days, too, summer activity often focuses on the waterfront – swimming, waterskiing, sailing, sunbathing. Indeed, today's residents may actually use the waterfront more intensively than in the past: In those times few private boating docks were to be seen, whereas today the shoreline is crowded with piers reaching out into the lake, with multiple lifts for motorized craft of all sorts.

Several communal activities of recent origin have helped create a new tradition. The Point Chautauqua picnic is a prominent example. This annual gathering brings together the families and guests of residents, makes possible the renewal of old friendships, and helps an increasingly diverse group of people become better acquainted with each other. The daylong festivities on picnic day include regattas, a marathon foot race through the streets of the community, and games and contests for persons of all ages.

Another regular occasion is the annual meeting of the Point Chautauqua Association, held annually on the first Saturday after the Fourth of July. At the end of the summer season, Point Chautauqua's residents again assemble at Memorial Park for the annual corn roast. A more recently established custom is the gala New Year's Eve party for year-round residents. Frederick Law Olmsted would have rejoiced to see the good fellowship and cordiality displayed at these gatherings [Point Chautauqua 1975, p. 1].

With arrival of the twenty-first century, community governance remains little changed from the pattern established in the early post-World War II period. The Point Chautauqua Association is still the main vehicle for common action by the residents who comprise its membership. The not-for-profit Land Company, together with its companion organization, the Point Chautauqua Water Company (with the same officers and directors), continues to own and operate the water-distribution system, parklands, various lakefront properties, and lots along Leet Avenue opposite the golf course. These are the lands received from the five heirs of Henry C. Fry upon his death in 1929. The Land Company leases its lakefront lots to Point Chautauqua residents for use as dock sites. The water system, a very old one acquired from The Inn shortly after the Second World War, is gradually being modernized. The Water Company draws its water from the lake, purifies it under State inspection, and distributes it during the warm seasons to summer residents lacking their own wells [Point Chautauqua 1975; Point Chautauqua Land and Water Companies 1991].

One of the most farsighted actions taken by community leaders in recent years was to obtain protection for Point Chautauqua under township zoning laws. In the late 1970s the community was designated a Residential District, which affords the greatest protection available. This category is restricted to single-family dwellings and a specified minimum lot size. Exceptions are made only for those structures already in place before the ordinance came into effect. Zoning protection arrived none too soon, for, as the quality of the community has improved in recent years, it has been under repeated attack from those attempting to gain variances for multi-family structures and for building on substandard lots. On each occasion the residents have joined in a body to resist any assault on the fundamental character of their Olmsted-designed community.

National Recognition

*M*ost residents of Point Chautauqua have always known that their colony was designed by Frederick Law Olmsted. But until recently only a few were fully aware of the preeminence of this pioneering landscape architect or of the rarity and historical significance of the community they had received from him. Only after authorities in historic landscape design chanced upon this little-known architectural gem did many who live here come to appreciate the true value of the Olmsted heritage.

THE NATIONAL REGISTER DRIVE

*T*his discovery came about in 1983 during the course of a statewide tour of Olmsted-designed sites by officials of the New York State Association for Olmsted Parks. They undertook the excursion to become better acquainted with these historic treasures and, in particular, to raise the general consciousness of New York's Olmsted legacy. It was therefore with considerable excitement that, while on the tour, one of the officials, Claire Ross of the New York State Department of Parks, Recreation, and Historic Preservation, came upon a copy of Olmsted's original design map for Point Chautauqua. She shared this find with Association for Olmsted Parks President Joan Bozer, who then arranged meetings with members of the community to alert them to the great historical value of their settlement.

89
❧

The Historical Preservation Committee

Accompanied by the Reverend Ralph Loew, head of the religion program at Chautauqua Institution and a person with keen interest in historical landscape architecture, Ms. Bozer spoke stirringly to Point Chautauquans and other interested persons on the imperative need to preserve this unique Olmsted design for future generations of Americans. A twofold plan evolved to address the need: The Chautauqua County Historical Society of Westfield agreed to take the steps necessary for Olmsted's Point Chautauqua design to be listed on the National Register of Historic Places. Meanwhile, the Point Chautauqua Association appointed an Historical Preservation Committee to develop a township preservation ordinance to provide local governmental protection for the surviving elements of the Olmsted plan.

With technical and legal help from the Preservation League of New York, the Historical Preservation Committee prepared a document for presentation by the president of the Point Chautauqua Association to the Town Board in 1987. Upon advice from the League's counsel, the submission actually took the form of a preservation resolution rather than an ordinance. The Town Board, however, decided to defer action on the matter until the community could obtain National Register listing. At this point, therefore, the Committee decided to take over the drive for National Register listing from the County Society in order to accelerate the effort.

The initial step in the National Register process was to prepare an application to the New York State Department of Parks, Recreation and Historic Preservation in Albany for listing on the New York State Register of Historic Places. To satisfy the exacting requirements of the Parks Department, Committee members undertook extensive research into the history of Point Chautauqua and the background and career of its designer, Frederick Law Olmsted. In addition, the Committee photocopied more than a hundred pages of Olmsted correspondence from the Library of Congress in Washington.

While this work was in progress, the Committee drew upon the advice and assistance of the Buffalo Friends of Olmsted, an established society devoted to the preservation of Buffalo's large Olmsted-designed park system. Committee members also attended meetings of the National Olmsted Society to develop an acquaintance among the devoted members of the group. Through these contacts, the Committee was able to enlist the help of one of the leading authorities on historic landscape architecture, Dr. Francis R. Kowsky, Professor of Art History at Buffalo State College, who provided invaluable counsel and guidance during the National Register drive. Through Dr. Kowsky, Committee members have also broadened their acquaintance with individuals and organizations active in historical preservation.

By the summer of 1992 the Committee had completed its initial application and on July 6th submitted this to the Albany office of the Parks Department, where it was enthusiastically received. Some weeks later an analyst and staff members from the department paid an inspection visit to Point Chautauqua. The inspectors noted approvingly the many Olmsted-designed roads still surviving in their original curvilinear pattern. They expressed disappointment, however, that so many of the public lands, with which Olmsted had so lavishly provided the community, had been diverted to other uses. They deplored the loss of the religious grounds and the Tabernacle site in particular.

The Historical Preservation Committee responded by pointing out that Point Chautauqua's early church-camp period had been merely a brief transitory phase and that religion had not proved to be a viable support base for community development. On the other hand, the Committee noted, the original Olmsted roads continued remarkably intact and remained as incomparable examples of the master's community-design principles. Furthermore, Point Chautauqua still possessed its half-mile stretch of waterfront, bordered by that unique feature of Olmsted design, The Strand – an open, grassy strip occupying the space between the water and the coastal road, Lake Avenue. Then, too, Fountain Park still existed in its pristine state, expressing the simple naturalness that is the hallmark of Olmsted's work. Overlooking the peninsula that gives Point

Chautauqua its name, this charming grassy triangle occupied one of the most prominent positions of all Olmsted's open lands. To be seen through its majestic grove of sugar maples was an incomparable view of the upper basin of Lake Chautauqua, a vista preserved in generations of souvenir prints and photographs.

Looking for support in making its case to the State, the Committee again turned to Dr. Kowsky. At this point he called upon another leading Olmsted scholar, Dr. Charles E. Beveridge of American University, editor of *The Papers of Frederick Law Olmsted,* for advice and help. In late October of 1992 these two eminent authorities visited Point Chautauqua and undertook a thorough survey of the community's road system and public lands, making direct measurements and comparing these with Olmsted's original design map. Upon completing their analysis, they declared that the existing road system and general layout of Point Chautauqua were indeed authentic Olmsted products, conforming unusually well to the master's initial plan. They concluded, therefore, that steps should be taken to preserve this Olmsted design, and that it should be listed on the National Register of Historic Places. Both wrote strong letters to the New York State Parks Department in support of the Committee's application.

Under urging from its sponsors, who recognized Point Chautauqua as a rare example of the master landscape architect's work, the following year the Committee took its case directly to the New York State Board for Historic Preservation, the ultimate decision-making body at the State level. In a presentation to the Board, which met in Albany on September 9, 1993, members of the Committee explained the unique features of this Olmsted-designed community. Board members responded favorably to the arguments and urged the Committee to press on with its National Register efforts. The Board also recommended that the Committee secure the services of a professional consultant experienced in this kind of preservation work to develop the formal submission.

Success

To pay for these consulting services, the Committee secured two grants: one from the New York State Council on the Arts and the other a Rural Grant under the Kaplan Fund, both administered by the Preservation League. Residents of Point Chautauqua generously contributed matching funds. Additional money was raised through bake sales held by children of Committee members and by the sale of copies of the Committee's Point Chautauqua booklet, souvenir T-shirts, sweatshirts, and duplicates of the Olmsted Point Chautauqua map. With financing in hand, the Committee secured the services of Barbara Campagna, a respected New York City consultant with local ties in western New York. Ms. Campagna prepared a formal submission, conducting fieldwork in the community with help from Committee members. Meanwhile, the Committee secured the valuable support of State political leaders, notably Senator Daniel Patrick Moynihan and local Assemblyman William Parment. In late 1995 Ms. Campagna presented the completed final application to the State. Word reached Point Chautauqua in March 1996 that the application had been approved, placing the community officially on the New York State Register of Historic Places. Listing on the National Register would follow in due course.

There followed on June 16, 1996, a festive celebration luncheon for all residents of Point Chautauqua at the nearby Sword and Shield Restaurant. In attendance were county and township officials and their wives, as well as members of the press and local historians. A place of special honor was reserved for Joan Bozer, President of the New York State Association for Olmsted Parks and the person who had first proposed that Point Chautauqua deserved a place on the National Register. J. Winthrop Aldrich III, New York State Deputy Commissioner of Parks, Recreation, and Historic Preservation, delivered the main address. Commissioner Aldrich concluded his talk by informing the group that National Register listing had also been approved. He presented the Committee chairperson with a certificate confirming this.

HISTORICAL PRESERVATION SOCIETY

*B*y the time the National Register listing was attained, the Committee had already undergone a fundamental change. Originally an ad hoc group appointed by the Point Chautauqua Association specifically to address the National Register project, the Committee reorganized as the Point Chautauqua Historical Preservation Society. On June 9, 1995, it became incorporated under the laws of the State of New York as a not-for-profit, tax-exempt, chartered society.

Society Aims

There were two main reasons for the change: first, it would help the community take advantage of new opportunities arising from the National Register listing. When undertaking fund drives, the Society could offer prospective donors tax exemptions for their contributions, an important aid to raising money. The new structure would be critcal to attracting grants, because donor agencies ordinarily require that funds be administered by tax-exempt entities.

Second, securing a State charter would increase the Society's ability to assume the new responsibilities resulting from National Register status. Now that its Olmsted design has gained official recognition as a national treasure, Point Chautauqua is obliged to preserve the design intact, not only for its own future residents but also for all citizens of the country. As the guardian of the Olmsted legacy, the Society is therefore charged with ensuring that all property owners and local officials are aware of the nature and value of the design and remaining vigilant in preventing any compromising of its historical character. See Box 1 for a complete list of the purposes of the Society as stated in the charter.

Box 1
PURPOSES OF THE
POINT CHAUTAUQUA HISTORICAL
PRESERVATION SOCIETY

a. To preserve the integrity of the community design of Point Chautauqua, located in the Town of Chautauqua, Chautauqua County, New York, as designed by Frederick Law Olmsted in 1875, through means including, but not limited to, obtaining listing on the National Register of Historic Places;

b. To disseminate and encourage a greater knowledge of the history of Point Chautauqua, New York, with particular reference to the work of its designer, Frederick Law Olmsted;

c. To gather, preserve, display, and make available for study artifacts, relics, books, manuscripts, papers, photographs, and other records and materials relating to the history of Point Chautauqua, New York, and the surrounding area;

d. To encourage the suitable marking of places of historic interest;

e. To acquire by purchase, gift, devise, or otherwise the title to or the custody and control of historic sites and structures, and to preserve and maintain such sites and structures;

f. To promote and encourage original historical and architectural research.

With the National Register listing achieved, the Society began addressing its new responsibilities, including the charge to mark places of historic interest. In 1999, therefore, the Society obtained a bronze plaque commemorating the listing of Point Chautauqua on the Register and mounted it on one of the two historic stone pillars standing at the upper entrance to the settlement. As a gift to the community, the Society also performed needed restoration work on both pillars, which had fallen into disrepair during the years that they had stood guard at that site. In addition, the group reinstalled the traditional pillar lights, which had remained dark in recent times. The photograph on p. 96

[Figure 42] shows the plaque in its place on the south pillar. Longtime residents of Point Chautauqua rejoiced at the mending of the entry pillars and restoration of their lights, which now serve as guiding beacons to welcome those returning to the settlement after nightfall. The prominent display of the National Register plaque is a source of great community pride and a continual reminder of their obligation to preserve this heritage.

Achievements

The Society has pursued its educational role along several avenues. Chief among these was the publication and distribution of its booklet *Olmsted's Point Chautauqua: The Story of an Historic Lakeside Community.* The work grew out of the

Figure 42 ❧ National Register plaque, mounted on a pillar at the entrance to the community. In 1996, following a concerted drive, Point Chautauqua gained recognition from the United States Department of the Interior for its well-preserved and historically important Frederick Law Olmsted design. This plaque, which commemorates the listing of the community on the National Register of Historic Places, is mounted on one of the traditional stone pillars standing guard at the upper entrance to Leet Avenue. To mark this occasion, the Historical Preservation Society repaired the aging twin pillars and restored their lights, which faithfully come on each evening at dusk to welcome returning residents.
❧ Photograph courtesy of Jane Currie

Committee's original National Register application to the State Parks Department. It has been amended and expanded at various times, with different versions distributed widely within the community and beyond to raise general awareness of Olmsted's Point Chautauqua design and its importance. This present book represents a substantial revision and development of the earlier work, though directed toward a wider audience. Other educational efforts of the Society include publishing newsletters on preservation matters for members of the Point Chautauqua community and providing occasional assistance to graduate students involved in research on historical landscape architecture.

In 1999 the Society introduced a new educational venture that has stirred much interest among residents of Point Chautauqua and the Chautauqua Lake region beyond: an annual series of lectures given by nationally prominent authorities on historic landscape architecture and general preservation matters. On Saturday, May 15th of that year, Dr. Frank Kowsky, who had played such a crucial part in securing Point Chautauqua's National Register listing, became the first lecturer in the series. Addressing a large audience of residents and their guests from neighboring parts of western New York, Dr. Kowsky discussed the fruitful collaboration between Calvert Vaux and Frederick Law Olmsted in the development of American landscape architecture. The leading authority on the career of Vaux and author of the critically acclaimed book *Country, Park and City*, Dr. Kowsky spoke to a rapt audience. So enthusiastic was the response to his talk that the Society prevailed upon him to deliver another address the following year. The illustrated talk, delivered on May 13th, dealt with the Hudson Valley landscape artists whom Olmsted and Vaux had known and who had influenced their park designs.

The discovery that Point Chautauqua was a rare and important Olmsted creation, followed by its listing on the National Register, has directed widespread attention to the community. Following his first visit to Point Chautauqua, Olmsted scholar Dr. Charles Beveridge added a section on Point Chautauqua to his next edition of *The Olmsted Papers*. Then, in 1994, two of Canada's leading art photographers, under commission from the Canadian Centre for Architecture in Montreal, visited Point Chautauqua to record scenes in the community. Later, in 1996 and 1997, the Centre included one of the photographs in an exhibit entitled "Frederick Law Olmsted in Perspective," which traveled to major cities in Canada and the United States [see Lambert 1996]. One of the Point Chautauqua scenes from the exhibit also appeared in an article, "Olmsted's Visions," in the magazine *Preservation* [Cole 1996].

Numerous visitors have come to Point Chautauqua in recent years to see firsthand its Olmsted design. One of these was Cynthia Zaitzetsky, who included the community on her tour of Olmsted creations in this part of the country. Ms. Zaitzetsky is the leading authority on Boston's Emerald Necklace park system, one of Olmsted's best-known designs [Zaitzetsky 1982]. On another occasion, members of the Buffalo Friends of Frederick Law Olmsted took a walking tour of Point Chautauqua. The community has also received visits from other individuals with a special interest in historical landscape architecture, including Joan Bozer and Clyde Peller, Co-Directors of the New York State Association for Olmsted Parks; Tania Werbizky of the Preservation League of New York; and Winthrop Aldrich III, Deputy Director of the New York State Department of Parks and Historic Preservation. Point Chautauqua also has become the subject of research by graduate students of historic landscape architecture.

Another opportunity for the Society to raise awareness of Point Chautauqua's heritage occurred in the autumn of 1999, when the U.S. Postal Service issued a special stamp commemorating Frederick Law Olmsted's career as a park builder. The local post office invited patrons in its large service area to a reception that served the combined purposes of inaugurating its new Dewittville building, introducing the new commemorative Olmsted stamp, and according special recognition to the rare Olmsted-designed community in its midst. At this occasion the postmistress presented the Historical Preservation Society with a large plaque displaying a replica of the Olmsted stamp. Afterward, the President of the Society spoke to this representative group of Chautauqua region residents on the nature and meaning of Olmsted's work at Point Chautauqua.

Challenges

As is often the case in historic communities, responsibility for maintaining historic sites has presented the Society with difficult challenges. Sensitive to the distressing loss, over many years, of so many of the public lands with which Olmsted had generously endowed the original Point Chautauqua, members of the Society responded eagerly to an opportunity to regain community control over the tract once occupied by the Tabernacle. The site had lain vacant, unkempt and overgrown by trees and underbrush since the old structure was razed shortly after the start of the last century. In 1996 the current owner of the site, who had previously been unwilling to sell, decided to put the property on the market. At its annual meeting that year, members of the Point Chautauqua Association voted overwhelmingly for the community to conduct a drive to raise the monies for its purchase. As a tax-exempt, not-for-profit corporation, the Historical Preservation Society agreed to accept donations and conduct negotiations. Despite strenuous efforts by the Society, however, another party bought the property, which is destined to be used as the site of a private dwelling.

Another provision in its charter calls for the Society to collect historically significant artifacts and make these available for study. This, however, has presented the problem of finding suitable quarters for housing such a collection, inasmuch as the community has been without public buildings since the end of the commercial era following World War II. As an interim solution, the Society has implemented a plan for keeping historic relics, books, photographs, and other artifacts in private homes. Acting as curator, a society member maintains a master list of the items and their locations. Interested persons – academic researchers, residents of Point Chautauqua, and others in the Chautauqua region – may consult the master list and, by special appointment, study these objects in the homes where they are kept.

The protection of public lands that still remain under community control has proved as difficult today as in the past. This became apparent when a committee of the Point Chautauqua Association chose one of the few remaining Olmsted-designed public areas, Fountain Park, as the site for a large formal design for a memorial to deceased residents. In recognition of Olmsted's antipathy to geometric patterns, as confirmed by communications on the subject from Drs. Kowsky and Beveridge, the Society conducted an information campaign to persuade Association members to find a less historically important location for the memorial. When the issue came up at the next annual meeting, however, the memorial proposal won by a bare three-vote margin. The centrality of the park, together with the strongly held feelings of some residents for a prominently located memorial – as well as the difficulty of communicating effectively with a largely seasonal population – were the deciding factors. Acknowledging the divided opinions on the issue, however, the Association sharply scaled back the size of the memorial and eliminated its formal design features. The Historical Society could take a measure of comfort, therefore, from the knowledge that its information campaign had resulted in a somewhat more tasteful and less-obtrusive object. Nevertheless, this sequence of events demonstrated the importance of ensuring that all Point Chautauqua's residents fully understand the rarity of the Olmsted design and that they remain alert to the necessity to protect and preserve it.

CHAPTER SEVEN

Point Chautauqua in
the New Century

*T*hat Point Chautauqua was created by the most influential of American landscape architects is an essential fact that needs to be recognized not only by community residents but also by local officials and dwellers of the Lake Chautauqua region at large. Moreover, if future generations are to see and experience this masterpiece of the nineteenth-century master designer, it is imperative that members of the present generation appreciate its fragility and be alert to the problems of preserving it undiminished for all time. Though we cannot know what hazards the future may bring, we must be attentive to the possible effects of population change and of technological, social, and political development.

A NATIONAL TREASURE

*T*hrough all the vicissitudes of the past century and a quarter, the greater part of Olmsted's original design for Point Chautauqua has somehow survived. In recognition of the eminence of its creator and the fact that his work largely endures here, the U.S. Department of the Interior has listed the community on the National Register of Historic Places. The Point Chautauqua design is widely acknowledged to be a rare example of the master planner's art and unique among his many works. Throughout the grounds are multiple examples of the celebrated Olmsted principles of landscape design. The community therefore remains a valuable artifact to be appreciated by its inhabitants and to be studied by future generations of landscape planners.

The Master Planner

Fundamental to Point Chautauqua's claims to distinction is the commanding position in nineteenth-century landscape architecture accorded its creator, Frederick Law Olmsted, whose work continues to exert a powerful influence today, both in the United States and throughout the world. Olmsted's contributions to the development of landscape design occupy a pivotal position in the history of that movement. This has been a clear line of progression, which began with Brown and Repton, acquired new dimensions with Olmsted, and evolved further with succeeding generations of Olmsted disciples.

To the physical standards of park planning developed in England, Olmsted added a new set of social goals, which became a central guiding force in his creative efforts. With his inherited love of natural beauty, he was receptive to the romantic treatment of the landscape that had become the distinguishing mark of English designers. And, as a product of the intellectual environment of his native New England, Olmsted was sympathetic to the egalitarian ideas of English social thinkers regarding the recreational needs of ordinary citizens. From his own varied life experience he was able to draw upon a body of practical knowledge, such as the physical properties of soils, and had a close acquaintance, based upon direct personal involvement, with the great social issues and movements of his day. Out of all these came the celebrated Olmsted principles of landscape design.

Credited with "bringing the garden into the city," Olmsted became the inspiration for generations of planners of parks and communities, as well as designers of houses, such as Frank Lloyd Wright. Nowhere has the impact of Olmsted's ideas been greater than in the garden-city and New Town movements in Britain, on the European continent, and in many other countries. Deeply impressed by Olmsted's plan for Riverside, Illinois, the English urban planner Ebenezer Howard developed a set of innovative concepts that has changed ideas about urban design throughout the world.

The visible record of Olmsted's creativity abounds in the United States, from his native New England to the shores of California. The National Association for Olmsted Parks has catalogued hundreds of these reminders of the master's genius. The NAOP's extraordinarily diverse master list of Olmsted projects includes parks, parkways, recreational areas, city and regional planning projects, subdivisions and suburban communities, college campuses, grounds of institutions and public buildings, monuments and statue designs, arboreta and gardens, and a great many other sites.[27] The master list also includes Point Chautauqua.

The Significance of Point Chautauqua as an Olmsted Design

When Olmsted agreed to prepare a design for Point Chautauqua's public lands and its roadway and lot systems, he had already produced plans for Central Park, Riverside, and Tacoma, and was at work on the Buffalo park system. He was therefore at the peak of his creativity, working alone following the dissolution of his partnership with Vaux, during a period when he was serving community leaders who were entirely sympathetic to his high purposes. By this time he had developed his fundamental design principles, and he proceeded to incorporate these into the Point Chautauqua plan.

The design problems he encountered at Point Chautauqua were both familiar and different. One characteristic that distinguished this project from the others was its setting: the new religious retreat was to occupy a slope descending sharply to the Lake Chautauqua shore. Indeed, as it turned out, Point Chautauqua was destined to become the only Olmsted-designed community perched on a steep hillside.[28] Another distinctive feature of the new settle-

---

[27] Altogether, Olmsted is credited with approximately 300 plans, in addition to the more than 3,000 projects undertaken by the Olmsted firm in the half-century following his retirement in 1895 – truly a prodigious output [Beveridge 1999].

[28] Though Olmsted's Tacoma design was likewise intended for a community situated on a steep slope rising from a large body of water, his plan for Tacoma was never carried out (see above).

ment was its prime function. Point Chautauqua was to be a religious community – a new kind of challenge for Olmsted. Secondarily, it was to serve both as a vacation retreat – a park – and as a residential community for those whose activities here extended throughout the summer season and beyond. Park designs and community designs had become fairly routine assignments for Olmsted by this time, but not in this combination.

It is of more than passing interest that, not long after it came into operation, Point Chautauqua's principal purpose – as a religious colony – became secondary, and eventually ceased altogether, while its other purposes – as a recreational and residential area – then became primary. Point Chautauqua's importance as an Olmsted design therefore derives not only from the imaginative way in which he met the novel demands of a religious retreat with a distinctive physical setting, but also the ingenuity with which he incorporated his cherished design principles into the planning of a residential community.

The Realization of Olmsted's Design Principles
Given full rein by the Point Chautauqua Association's Baptist ministers and lay leaders to fashion the new design in accordance with his own criteria, Olmsted proceeded to replace his clients' preconceived notions with a plan that embodied his own principles.[29] The Olmsted precepts survive today at Point Chautauqua in both their physical and social aspects. The exceptional degree to which he succeeded in embedding these lofty ideals into the enduring fabric of the community remains one of the chief claims for Point Chautauqua's recognition as a prime example of Olmsted's work.

Provided with a physical landscape of the kind he most preferred – a forested slope rising steeply above a beautiful body of water – Olmsted emphatically rejected the suggestion of a conventional grid pattern for his roadways. In the tradition of Capability Brown, he chose instead to follow the

---

[29] Olmsted's ability to alter the thinking of Point Chautauqua's leaders in such a fundamental manner demonstrates clearly the great respect with which he had come to be regarded and illustrates his substantial role in shaping the aesthetic tastes of America's elite.

lay of the land, thereby avoiding steep ascents of the kind found at Fair Point across the lake. The long entranceways created by crescent-shaped Leet Avenue not only shield residents from the heavily traveled highway but also prevent the community from sprawling along this route in the manner so common elsewhere around the lake. At the same time, Leet Avenue can be viewed as Point Chautauqua's connecting link with the faraway crowded urban centers from which tired workers come to this retreat for recuperation. Thus, in typical Olmsted manner, a very practical arrangement yields social benefits.

Indeed, Point Chautauqua's physical layout owes its main features to the aesthetic and social values so firmly held by their designer. The winding roadways offer relief from the bland sameness of conventional gridiron plans but, at the same time, yield Olmsted's famed "mysteries" and create endless sylvan vistas [Figure 43]. The curvilinear form of the roadways results in the delightful triangular grassy plots seen at intersections. Similarly, Olmsted arranged his lots in such a way that, as the roads wind in parallel, step-wise fashion up the slopes, every dwelling might enjoy a sweeping view of Chautauqua valley. Further enhancing this prospect is the wide spacing of the houses, consistent with Olmsted's abhorrence of crowding, of "houses set down meanly side by side."[30]

Though determined to avoid unwholesome cramped living conditions, Olmsted nevertheless believed that community plans should support interaction among diverse groups of people by providing open common lands that bring the inhabitants together [Stevenson 1977, p. 329]. His design for Point Chautauqua accomplished this abundantly and with much success. The arterial routes leading from the twin entrances on Leet Avenue funnel traffic

---

[30] It will be noted that Olmsted's lots were individually small, consistent with his original charge to provide spaces for the large number of tents to be pitched by those attending the planned Bible camp. The large green spaces separating today's substantial houses result from the general practice of putting together several of Olmsted's lots for each dwelling. This change in the land-use pattern was a logical response to the abrupt termination of Point Chautauqua's religious function. Given Olmsted's often-stated views on the evils of crowding, it is obvious that he would have readily endorsed this change.

Figure 43 ❧ An Olmsted "mystery" in winter. After one of Point Chautauqua's heavy snowfalls, the woodland vistas that appear unexpectedly around bends in the road can be strikingly beautiful. Though the community was designed as a summer colony, a few families have always lived here year-round and have learned to expect snowfalls that may total 300 inches or more in a season. Frigid winter winds blowing out of the northwest pick up immense quantities of moisture as they cross the open waters of Lake Erie and deposit it as snow as they rise over the Allegheny highlands in the lee of the lake. Point Chautauqua is therefore a place to enjoy the beauty of every season: the wispy green leaf buds and wildflower-covered forest floors of spring, the deep shade of tree-lined walks and sunny expanses of blue water of summer, and the magnificent blaze of brilliant foliage in autumn, followed by the pristine white blanket of winter.   ❧ Photo by Joan Hicks

into the central area where Olmsted placed the Tabernacle grounds and the other large open areas intended to further the community's initial religious objectives. From this convergence at the old Tabernacle site, the movement of pedestrians and vehicles is drawn directly to the beach by way of Emerald and Diamond Avenues (see Walking Tour, Appendix A). Point Chautauqua's extensive waterfront – together with the bordering Strand and Lake Avenue and the adjacent Fountain Park – makes up a substantial portion of the community's open space. Beyond this, the great sweep of Lake Chautauqua's ever-changing seascape and the distant vista of the forested Allegheny foothills rising in ranks above the distant shore – these give a sense of being wholly enveloped by natural beauty.

Thus, in his original plan Olmsted provided Point Chautauqua with a profusion of park and recreational areas, surely more green spaces in relation to its size and population than in any of his usual community plans. However, Olmsted conceived Point Chautauqua in different terms from his other communities. Given the mission of its founders, it was to perform a multiplicity of functions, each of which carried its own space requirements. The loss of its primary religious purpose substantially diminished the need for central assembly areas. Consequently, that portion of Ashmore Park still remaining, now called Memorial Park, serves the outdoor assembly needs of today's ninety-some households: the annual picnic, the corn roast, the festivals and sporting events. These occasions respond to Olmsted's desire for central areas that support "interaction among diverse groups of people." Point Chautauqua's immensely popular communal gatherings effectively bridge the gaps that might otherwise separate a population that is now of far greater diversity than in its religious past. Sons and daughters of Point Chautauqua regularly arrange their vacation times and military leaves in such a way that they can return for these annual reunions with the friends with whom they grew up.

From the beginning, however, the day-to-day meeting place of Point Chautauqua's people has been the half-mile middle section of its waterfront. In more leisurely times, families and friends assembled in groups along the

Figure 44 ❧ Contemporary view of the waterfront from the air. Point Chautauqua's shoreline has undergone much change in recent years. Gone are the tracks and overhead wires of the trolley. All that remains of the old right-of-way is a slight grass-covered ridge beside Lake Avenue and a stretch of barely visible railway ties at the Elm Park site. Gone, too, are all the traces of the once-thriving commercial center at the old boat landing. Prominent in this recent photo are the innumerable private docks now lining the shore, evidence of the immense popularity of boating in the present era. Conspicuous, too, is the popular outdoor meeting place and playing field that now occupies the southern end of Olmsted's former Ashmore Park.   ❧ Photo by John Sirianno

shore each morning and remained there through most of the afternoon. Today it is mainly the children who spend their days at the shore, in the safeguarded swimming area or at the waterfront playground. Aside from a daily dip in the lake, adults are more likely to be sailing in their boats. Thus Point Chautauqua's long lakefront area represents a large space devoted to open-air activities of the kind Olmsted sought to promote [Figure 44].

108
❧

On the whole, Olmsted's design for Point Chautauqua has proved resilient. After a century and a quarter his roadway system remains little altered, its sweeping curves still imparting the same pleasurable visual impact and restful feeling that they offered earlier generations [Figure 45]. Surely the atmosphere of comforting naturalness that attracted such a diverse group of people has also helped them achieve the congeniality and spirit of community that Olmsted

Figure 45 ⁓ Emerald Avenue gracefully winding through a winter landscape. The sweep of Olmsted's roadways at Point Chautauqua is best revealed after summer foliage has gone. In recent years more and more houses have been winterized so that they can be comfortably occupied in all seasons. In addition to the growing number of families living here around the year, many residents return on weekends and holidays to enjoy skiing and other winter sports abundantly available in the Chautauqua region. Diligent township crews keep the roadways well plowed for the school buses.   ⁓ Photo by Joan Hicks

always sought to achieve. Such a place, he said, "should be rural, natural, tranquilizing and poetic in character" [quoted in Stevenson 1977, p. 282]. This is the mood of Point Chautauqua, as any who have experienced it will confirm. Certainly it is a feeling that is unlike that of any other community throughout the Lake Chautauqua region.

Frederick Law Olmsted's Point Chautauqua admirably demonstrates the master's design principles [Box 2]. As a priceless work of art, it is to be cherished by all its inhabitants. As a one-of-a-kind gem of historic landscape architecture, recognized by the U. S. Department of the Interior, it is to be prized by all American citizens. As the product of the most influential designer of the nineteenth century, it stands as a valuable object for study by historians and future planners.

Box 2

THE OLMSTED PRINCIPLES OF DESIGN

✢   *Naturalness – the guiding theme of Olmsted's 37-year career.* Born to a family captivated by natural beauty, and growing up amidst the scenic beauty of the Connecticut Valley, he was convinced of the restorative powers of the natural landscape and its humanizing influence on all those it touched. Public green spaces are central to the unity and social progress of a community. Olmsted opposed all artificiality, as seen in his contempt for the "tortured shrubs" of the formal gardens he had visited in continental Europe. "Decorative gardening," that is, flower gardening, should be visually separated from those parts of the grounds that form the broader landscape.

✢   *Conforming to the natural lay of the land.* Because of his profound respect for nature, Olmsted steadfastly avoided inflexible, arbitrary design forms. His roads and public spaces appear to grow out of the terrain itself. Roadways follow the contour of the land, descending the steepest slopes with gentle gradients.

✢   *Curvilinear forms with unexpected vistas.* Olmsted was firmly opposed to the conventional grid street patterns favored by Western cities since Roman times. Instead, taking his inspiration from the pioneering English designers, Olmsted introduced twists and turns into his roadways. Around each bend, therefore, appears a surprising new vista – a "mystery," as Olmsted called it. This induces a comforting sense of enclosure and intimacy that is lacking in the traditional rectangular layout. Mindful of their socializing function, Olmsted planned his roads so as to converge upon natural meeting places.

✢   *Common lands that bring people together.* Centrally located meeting places are invariable features of Olmsted's community designs. These open spaces offer congenial natural surroundings where people can gather and strengthen the sense of community.

✢   *Restful sylvan retreats from the crowded city.* Olmsted endowed his communities with natural settings in which people could recover from the stresses of the workplace and crowded city living. For these rural retreats he recommended a minimum lot size of one acre, which would surround each family with an abundance of comforting green space. Olmsted insisted, however, that such communities be connected to the civilizing influence of cities.

Olmsted's vision was not a static one. Living in a dynamic era himself, he was aware of the inevitable effects of new technologies and social change on the inhabitants of a place. He therefore recommended periodic review of a community's design and the implementing of indicated modifications in response to new conditions. It is imperative, however, that any such changes be made in conformity with his basic design principles.

THE VULNERABLE OLMSTED DESIGN

*D*espite the durability of Olmsted's work at Point Chautauqua and the national recognition it has earned, its survival remains at risk. True, much of the original design remains intact more than a century and a quarter after its creation. The roads in particular have endured, largely in their original configuration. Clinging to its wooded slope above the lake, the community still conveys a sense of spaciousness and serene natural beauty. Yet even a casual acquaintance with Point Chautauqua's past leaves an unsettling impression that historical accident has played a large part in the community's ability to preserve much of value from those earlier days. Too often it was a fortunate combination of circumstances that averted harm to the Olmsted concept. From the outset the design was vulnerable, and it still is.

The Uses of Adversity

Paradoxically, the ability of Olmsted's artfully conceived road system to survive for 125 years owes much to the hard times that fell upon the settlement during the middle third of the twentieth century. The same circumstances had the effect also of reducing the community's population density, which even today remains much lower than in many other settlements around the lake. The reduced pressure on land supply helped preserve the green spaces for which Point Chautauqua is noted.[31]

111

---

[31] In more recent times the County Health Department has come to the rescue with its sanitary code, which specifies that every dwelling dependent upon its own septic system must have a lot of at least 200 square feet. Building permits are routinely denied because of inadequate lot size. Thus, once again, a fortuitous circumstance – public policy – has helped preserve Point Chautauqua's green spaces.

When economic conditions worsened during the Great Depression, fewer families made their annual visit to Point Chautauqua, a trend that accelerated during the Second World War and continued into the early postwar period. Neglected properties fell into decay; inns, hotels, and boarding houses were no longer able to attract sufficient customers and were forced to close. Unexplained fires consumed many of those abandoned structures. As open spaces grew up in weeds and underbrush, the settlement acquired a run-down appearance. Those who remember that era speak of the seedy look that discouraged prospective buyers of property. Vacant houses went unsold at any price. Such conditions provided no incentive for change, so Olmsted's curving roads – little used, unpaved, and concealed by a protective covering of undergrowth – remained unnoticed and safe from alteration.

Misspent Assets

But if adversity sheltered Olmsted's road system, hard times perversely affected his public lands. With the community's population dwindling and its resource base shrinking, the governing body of that day, the Public Service Association, soon found its finances depleted. For a time the few remaining residents of means supplied funding to keep the community afloat, but ultimately their efforts were unsuccessful. One nagging drain was the community's nine-hole golf course, which in better times had been laid out on adjacent lands to the north. When the golf course failed during the early 1940s, some of its supporters managed to retrieve their interests in the venture by gaining title to desirable parcels of the community's public lands. In this way one investor was able to acquire a particularly choice piece of waterfront land at the southern end of Olmsted's Strand. Though The Strand had always been regarded as inviolate – a recreational area specifically reserved by Olmsted for the enjoyment of all residents – this misappropriation went unchallenged at a time when community attention was focused upon survival.

It was during this period that the most grievous loss of historically important public lands occurred. Having run up very large legal fees, especially in the struggle to keep control of the golf course, the Association in desperation deeded over to its lawyer several large tracts. Among the prime holdings alienated in this way were the now-vacant Tabernacle site, together with the grounds Olmsted had designated for the Corinthian and Sylvan Groves. Ownership of these valuable lands continued to pass down through the hands of the lawyer's heirs until recently, when they were sold for private development despite community efforts to save them.

In an era when choice waterfront property is the most sought-after commodity throughout the Lake Chautauqua region today, The Strand remains the most vulnerable part of the community's Olmsted heritage. From the very beginnings of settlement, this slender strip of land has offered tempting locational advantages for all sorts of enterprises, especially transport activities. Indeed, Olmsted's original plan had provided docking space for large lake steamers on a small peninsula at the center of the Strand. During the resort era another facility was created for off-loading coal for heating dwellings, hotels, and other commercial establishments.

As we have seen, the Strand later became the location for the electric trolley line [refer to Figure 37]. By right of eminent domain, the railway company held title to the immediate right-of-way, which was left dormant after the line was abandoned. Thereafter, a public-spirited resident of substantial means purchased the trolley right-of-way and deeded it over to the newly established Point Chautauqua Land Company with the provision that it be administered for the good of the community. Despite this admonition, choice lakefront lots have continued to fall into private hands. One important piece of waterfront land lost in this manner was Olmsted's small Elm Park, at the northern end of the Strand.[32]

113

---

[32] The alienation of public spaces during the mid-twentieth century was, of course, not the first to occur at Point Chautauqua. Recall that one of the initial acts of the original Point Chautauqua Association in 1876 had been to convert Olmsted's Ashmore Park into a space for the aptly named Grand Hotel. In a bid to outdo their rivals at Fair Point across the Lake, the founding fathers abandoned their original modest plans and put up this immense structure in an area previously intended for the pitching of tents. Following destruction of the hotel by fire in 1902, much of the space it had occupied came to be used for private housing. The remainder ultimately became the playing field and outdoor meeting place for Point Chautauqua residents.

The long history of this community has been marked by profligate treatment of its public spaces. As a result, little of the community land with which Olmsted so generously endowed Point Chautauqua remains in its pristine state today. Not only has this loss of public space deprived residents of the beautifully natural parklands intended for their enjoyment, but it has diminished the historical integrity of the original Olmsted plan.

Indeed, it was on these grounds that officials of the New York State Department of Parks, Recreation and Historic Preservation initially declined to consider the community's petition for listing on the Register of Historic Places. Point Chautauqua eventually secured this listing only because leading Olmsted authorities pointed out to State authorities the rarity of the community's remarkably well-preserved road system and its distinction as the only Olmsted settlement laid out on a hillside overlooking a large body of water. They noted also that this setting had provided the master with an incomparable opportunity to demonstrate, in an area of steep slopes, his principle of laying out roads according to the underlying contour of the land.

Enduring Features

Despite its vicissitudes, Point Chautauqua continues to bear the unmistakable stamp of the master landscape architect. Much of Olmsted's design remains, still remarkably faithful to his original: The great majority of the roads – at least a dozen of them – still follow their Olmsted-prescribed contours, still curving with the landscape, still yielding new vistas around each bend, still converging upon the main assembly areas. No longer a religious colony, Point Chautauqua has long since replaced the tents of the faithful with substantial single-family dwellings, widely separated and surrounded with the green spaces Olmsted would have required of a residential community.[33]

114

---

[33] Recall that in his writings Olmsted specified one acre as the appropriate lot size for a residence. This standard still prevails in his most famous residential community, Riverside, Illinois.

Figure 46 ❧ Artist's conception of the former Point Chautauqua boat landing as it appears today. This tranquil view of the present waterfront – with its beached sailboats and martin house – offers no hint of the bustling scene at this location during Point Chautauqua's pleasure resort era, when this was the site of a busy commercial center, steamboat landing, and electric interurban stop (compare with Figures 29 and 30). ❧ From a sketch by Jane Nelson

What is more, because it remains essentially as Olmsted planned it, the road system in its present pattern effectively serves to keep intact the original form of the community as a whole. Indeed, the road pattern clearly defines the shapes of the lost public spaces. Nor has private ownership of the former public lands detracted materially from the natural beauty and spaciousness intended by Olmsted. Though many of the waterfront lots are in private hands, Olmsted's Strand is largely uncluttered with structures and thus continues to provide an unrestricted view of the waterfront [Figure 46]. Fountain and Elm Parks no longer remain in their original undefiled state, but both still offer magnificent vistas of the upper basin of beautiful Lake Chautauqua. Though privately owned, the Corinthian and Sylvan Groves are still heavily wooded and continue to supply a natural forest floor cover of shrubs and wildflowers.

SAVING POINT CHAUTAUQUA
FOR FUTURE GENERATIONS

*C*an we be confident that Point Chautauqua will remain as green in the future as it is today and that its open spaces will always be accessible to public view despite private ownership? Sadly, past experience offers little assurance on this point. History has shown that circumstances change with disconcerting suddenness, as happened in the case of the lost Tabernacle site. In the absence of firm community oversight, private decisions can speedily convert a natural landscape into a suburban-type property development. Preserving the special character of historic Point Chautauqua for the enjoyment and education of future generations requires clear recognition of the special dangers that confront this incomparable historic artifact.

Problems of Preservation

Nearly everywhere that it is undertaken, historical preservation seems to encounter obstacles. The problems are all the more troublesome if the design embodies a set of principles as idealistic as those of Frederick Law Olmsted. Olmsted himself discovered the difficulty of defending his very first product, the Olmsted/Vaux plan for Central Park, against the intrusion of incompatible land uses even before construction had been completed. Buffalo's superb Olmsted-designed park system has suffered grievous damage from the encroachment of multi-lane expressways, and the famous Boston Emerald Necklace chain of parks has been badly degraded. In addition to the usual issues of preservation, however, saving Olmsted's Point Chautauqua has presented special problems because of its particular circumstances. The gradual alienation of this community's public lands over the past century and a quarter illustrates these well.

From the outset, the Baptist clerics and lay leaders of the original Point Chautauqua Association misjudged their situation and made poor management decisions. At the community's 50th anniversary convocation, an early director, H. C. Fry, described his colleagues as "individually of great energy and sincerity, but perhaps somewhat deficient as financiers" [Point Chautauqua 1975]. Their stewardship ended with collapse of the religious mission and early bankruptcy for the commercial ventures with which they tried to replace it.

Despite their mistakes, these early leaders were mindful of their Olmsted heritage and were proud of it. With their passing, however, this lore perished, too. Older residents who are able to recall the ensuing period tell us that "Olmsted was just a name" to later generations. Only after Olmsted authorities had discovered this community's historic origins did many of the residents come to appreciate the importance of their inheritance. This lack of awareness of an illustrious history is not peculiar to Point Chautauqua. It is a familiar situation among historic communities generally, and especially those lacking a formal enforcement structure of the kind that has served Riverside, Illinois, so well.

Maintaining historical awareness faces an additional hurdle at Point Chautauqua: the seasonal nature of its population. From the outset this community was conceived as a summer colony, one of the many resorts ringing the 58-mile circumference of the lake. It was religious fervor that motivated the first settlers, not an appreciation for landscape architecture, however illustrious the designer. With the passing of the brief Bible-camp era, Point Chautauqua became a place for relaxation and entertainment. In those times people came to enjoy boating, swimming, and socializing in the mild comfort of the beautiful Allegheny foothills, just as they do today.

This is not to say that such incentives as these are inimical to Olmsted's design principles; indeed, one of his stated aims for such a plan was to provide the restorative benefits of a congenial natural setting. Nevertheless, it is hardly to be expected that summer visitors will necessarily arrive here with a knowledge of the careful planning to which they owe these pleasures, or of the stature that history has given the planner.

A seasonal population may also have other reasons for not immediately recognizing the value of the features that distinguish an Olmsted community. As new residents in Chautauqua, they will at first find Olmsted's open landscape a pleasant change from city congestion, but in time may come to miss their customary urban conveniences. They may be tempted to fill their unoccupied land with amenities of the kinds that they enjoy in winter.

This desire to be surrounded with familiar urban comforts is inimical to the Olmsted concept of widely spaced dwellings surrounded by broad green areas. In the preservation of this Olmsted ideal the community has benefited from the restrictive zoning secured by the foresightedness of a wise earlier generation, reinforced by the existence of a fortunate public sanitary code. As a result, Point Chautauqua continues to enjoy an open environment that contrasts markedly with the crowding that characterizes many other areas around the lake.

The impersonality of contemporary city life also tends to foster social attitudes unsuited to the ways of a summer colony. City folk are accustomed to controlling their own living spaces and are ever prepared to defend these from encroachment. At Point Chautauqua such an outlook may lead a property owner to erect a building or install plantings that make a neighbor feel crowded. In taking this action he may dismiss the neighbor's resentment, reasoning that he has a right to do what he pleases with his own property. If the installation also happens to cut off a much-cherished view of the lake, the rancor grows all the deeper. The neighbor's indignation is likely to be shared widely among Point Chautauqua's residents, who value open green spaces and, most particularly, an unobstructed lake vista.

Indeed, glorious Lake Chautauqua contributes much to that feeling of spaciousness relished by the inhabitants of this settlement. The sight of that great expanse of blue water fills them with a special sense of liberation. From the beginning Olmsted foresaw this very human feeling and therefore configured his roads in such a way that as many residents as possible would have a

lake prospect. This emotion pervades the community and finds its most force-
ful expression in property values. Lakefront properties command by far the
highest prices. Those not directly on the lake also enjoy a premium, though
substantially less, if they have an unobstructed view of it. Thus an action that
in any way impairs the sight of water is financially damaging to the affected
owners. In this new environment, therefore, city-bred residents are wise to
develop a keen sensitivity for their neighbors' interests.

As Point Chautauqua's prosperity has grown, as households have experienced generational change, and as the demand for choice lakeside residences
has surged, the turnover of properties has accelerated. Given the soaring prices
for lakeside lots, the purchasers are necessarily prosperous people, whose
arrival has caused average income levels to rise in the settlement. Moreover,
the addition of new residents year by year has led to greater population
diversity. Of the ninety-some families in residence in the year 2000, nearly a
quarter have arrived within the past five years. The newcomers have taken
their place among the substantial number of families who have lived here for
several generations. Seventeen families have been in residence fifty years or
more, and of these, twelve have been here for seventy-five years and three for
more than a century. Within the community, therefore, are widely contrasting
experiences with country living.

Despite Point Chautauqua's growing diversity, however, no clear divisions
are evident between the attitudes of longtime residents and those of the
newcomers. Many of the new arrivals have demonstrated an eagerness to learn
more about the Olmsted heritage. Some of the most ardent enthusiasts for
restoring the settlement's historic architectural gems are to be found among
those who have come to the community only recently.

This indicates the importance of acquainting residents with the community's
unique origins at the earliest possible moment. To promote this aim, local
realtors have been instructed concerning the value of the Point Chautauqua's
Olmsted design, and some of these use the information very productively as a

sales pitch to prospective clients. Then, when new owners take up actual residence, members of the Historical Preservation Society follow up with supplementary historical information. Introducing new property owners to their unique historical heritage in this manner lays an effective foundation for building an awareness of the need to preserve Point Chautauqua.

THE OBLIGATION TO PRESERVE

Considering the vulnerability of Olmsted's design for Point Chautauqua, as confirmed by past losses of community lands, it is essential that everyone associated with the community be convinced of the obligation to preserve what remains of it. This responsibility rests not only on the current owners of property but also on local township and county officials, especially those charged with enforcing zoning ordinances and maintaining the road system.

The residents who enjoy the grace and beauty of Point Chautauqua today need to be reminded of their debt to those early leaders who had the wisdom to engage America's most eminent landscape architect to plan their community. They must also be made to appreciate their obligation to preserve the Olmsted design for the pleasure and instruction of future generations.

Who are the expected beneficiaries of such preservation? First of all, today's residents should wish to assure survival of the community for the enjoyment of their own children and grandchildren. Preservation of the Olmsted design is important, too, for the people who live in and around the Lake Chautauqua Basin, where Point Chautauqua is the sole example of the master's work. Saving the design is clearly essential to the community of architectural scholars, for whom Point Chautauqua is the single example of an Olmsted-planned religious colony, and the one instance where Olmsted was able to apply his technique for accommodating a road pattern to a hillside location. Perhaps most basic of all, however, is the obligation of today's residents to future generations of all American citizens, whose government has officially affirmed the historic importance of Point Chautauqua.

It has been said that good community designs endure because they exert a beneficial influence over their inhabitants. As one who grew up in Point Chautauqua remarked upon returning to take up permanent year-round residence in her family's summer house of several generations, "This place was magical when I was a kid, and it still is. When you get home from work, you feel like you're on vacation. If you've had a stressful day at work, it falls right off you." If the test of an Olmsted design is its effectiveness in attaining social objectives, therefore, Point Chautauqua can truly be judged a success. The artifact that Olmsted used to produce this result, the community system of roadways and public spaces, has done its work well.

APPENDIX

A *Walking Tour of*
Point Chautauqua

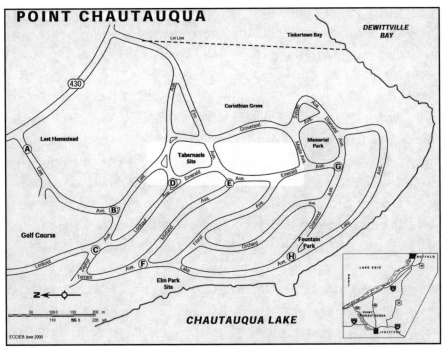

Figure 47 ❧ Walking-tour map of Point Chautauqua. Letters in brackets indicate reference points cited in the text.
❧ Map by Emil Boasson, Computer Cartography Laboratory, Department of Geography, SUNY/Buffalo

*W*ithout doubt, the best way to become truly acquainted with Point Chautauqua is to take a leisurely walk along Olmsted's winding roads and paths, pausing frequently to inspect the Victorian houses and admire the superlative views of the lake to be seen through openings in the trees. Occasionally during the course of our tour we shall consult the attached map [Figure 47][34].

34 Bracketed letters in the text correspond to key reference points indicated on the map.

123
❧

We enter Point Chautauqua through the lighted stone pillars marking the upper main entrance [A] and proceed along Leet Ave., which is bordered on our right by the golf course. Fringing the roadway on the left is a line of pin oak trees growing at intervals within a broad grassy strip.

Approaching the principal residential area, we become aware that this long, crescent-shaped drive effectively separates Point Chautauqua from the highway. This serves to shelter the community and also to prevent it from expanding outward to the highway and beyond. As in most parts of the nation, populated areas in the Lake Chautauqua region have tended to develop as parallel blocks adjacent to rural highways. It was this conventional, uninspired grid pattern that Olmsted was determined to defeat in his design for Point Chautauqua. One such grid design exists at Chautauqua Institution, a community of similar origins across the lake from Point Chautauqua. It is instructive to observe the markedly different layouts of these two settlements and to sense the contrasting moods they produce. The sheltering entrance drive is a common feature of private estates and parks in England and America, and this device has admirably served communities designed by Olmsted.

Continuing along Leet Ave. into the residential area, we come upon the first tributary street, Zephyr Avenue [B]. This branches off abruptly to the right and, bending gradually, descends to a lower elevation. A hundred feet or so along this roadway, we come upon a striking view of Lake Chautauqua. Seen through a broad opening in the trees, this vista overlooks a grassy expanse that descends steeply to the wooded shoreline. The trees framing the foreground are mainly maples, very old ones, which in fall turn brilliant shades of red, yellow, and orange – some of the choicest autumn colors in all of Western New York. The nearby trees have been planted far apart in the style Olmsted approved. He insisted that this wide spacing allowed each tree to have room for stretching out its branches.

As we advance along Zephyr toward its intersection with Lookout Avenue [C], the road drops sharply. Off to the right, Lookout Avenue continues along

Figure 48 ❧ An Olmsted-designed grassy triangle at the intersection of Leet and Emerald Avenues. Because of the curving nature of Olmsted's roadways, the places where they meet do not form square corners but instead assume the characteristic triangular aspect seen here. These features enhance the amount of green space at Point Chautauqua and thus contribute to its serenity. ❧ From a sketch by Jane Nelson

the southwest border of the golf course, passing on the left a row of houses perched on a steep wooded bluff with a magnificent view of the upper basin of Lake Chautauqua. There, at the northernmost margin of Point Chautauqua, the road ends.

Retracing our route, we follow Lookout beyond its intersection with Zephyr [C], where it enters beneath a dense canopy of maple trees shading several Victorian-era houses, some still retaining their overhanging porches and ornate trim. Lookout Avenue curves slightly to the left and rises gently toward a junction with Emerald Avenue. Where the two roads meet is a grassy triangle. Such triangles, with their neatly tended flower beds, are familiar features at Point Chautauqua road junctions [Figure 48].

At this spot [D], we are facing east, toward the areas where Olmsted placed the public portion of Point Chautauqua, on gently sloping land. On the highest ground he located the two assembly areas: the Tabernacle (an enclosed structure) and the Pavilion (open air). Downhill from the assembly areas were parklands: Corinthian and Sylvan Groves – tree-covered and laced with paths – and Ashmore Park – open and bordered by a walk. At the foot of Ashmore Park was a plot designated for a small hotel and refectory. Olmsted laid out Lake Avenue parallel to the shoreline and designated the narrow strip of land between the roadway and the waterfront , called The Strand, as a public area open to all residents of the community. The only features constructed on The Strand were the docks accommodating Lake Chautauqua's large steamboats, the principal means of transportation in a time of primitive overland travel.

The Tabernacle survived into the early 1900s, now beyond the memory of even the oldest residents. Until very recently the site was overgrown with trees and shrubs, in the center of which remained a small pond filled with peepers that sang on mild spring evenings. Apparently the Pavilion was never constructed; no traces or records of its physical existence have come to light. In 1876, the very year of Point Chautauqua's founding, community leaders converted the upper end of Ashmore Park into a site for the Grand Hotel, the largest such establishment in the region at that time. In 1902 this magnificent structure was lost to arson, and during the next half-century most of the other hotels in the settlement either burned or were torn down. Today the only part of the original Ashmore Park still surviving is a lower section, now called Memorial Park. This continues to serve the recreational needs of the residents. It features tennis courts, basketball courts, a baseball diamond, and a picnic area, where each July the residents hold the annual Point Chautauqua Picnic – with games, races, and contests – and where they celebrate the end of summer with a corn roast.

Continuing our walk from point **D,** we follow Emerald Avenue as it bends around the Tabernacle site and descends toward Midland Avenue **[E]**. We turn sharply to the right into Midland, which follows the contour of the land as it takes a downward winding course toward its intersection with Terrace and Floral Avenues [F]. Here, looking out across a grassy triangle of land that Olmsted had designated as Elm Park, we enjoy a sweeping view of the lake through the towering maple trees that now occupy the site. We turn right on Terrace and ascend steeply to Zephyr Avenue. Here the Olmsted plan called for a northwestern extension of Terrace. This road was laid out but has now fallen into disuse.

A sharp right turn onto Zephyr takes us up a steep and curving incline, until once again we find ourselves at the juncture of Lookout and Zephyr Avenues. Lookout and Terrace Avenues were the only roads actually laid out at this end of Point Chautauqua. The original plan called for extensions of Lake Avenue and another roadway called Highland, but these were never constructed.

Now we retrace our steps downhill, back along Zephyr. Returning to the spot where Zephyr meets Terrace, we encounter at middle height a splendid view of the lake and the wooded hills, rising in tiers above the opposite shore, two miles away. On still, clear nights, hundreds of lights from distant Mayville, a town set on a high hill, glow and send their reflections across the waters. All along these upper roadways of Point Chautauqua, passersby can catch frequent glimpses of the lake and its far shore. Many residents are able to enjoy these enchanting scenes from their own porches and windows, benefiting from Olmsted's ingenuity in arranging the lots so that most houses look out upon the lake.

Walking downward along Terrace, again we reach its junction with Midland and Floral Avenues [F]. As we proceed along Floral, we descend steeply for a short distance, then climb again, past the intersection with Orchard Avenue and on to the end of Floral at its junction with Emerald. Like Midland and Orchard, which it parallels, Floral offers a series of graceful S-shaped curves. With only a few exceptions, the houses lining Floral and Orchard Avenues were built in the 1870s and 1880s, very soon after Olmsted's plan was implemented.

Turning right from Floral onto Emerald, again we pass, this time on the left, the tract that Olmsted designated as Ashmore Park. Today this area is bisected by Maple Avenue. Clearly Olmsted did not design this short, straight road, because it lacks the customary curves. It is one of only two non-original roads in the entire settlement. On our right, in an area now occupied by houses, is the former site of another notable Point Chautauqua hostelry, The Inn, which continued to thrive as a community social center well into the middle of the twentieth century. As we continue down Emerald, we pass Memorial Park and soon reach the junction of Emerald with Diamond Avenue [G]. We then turn right and proceed along Diamond, past the intersection of Diamond and Orchard. Beyond, the road declines gradually toward the lake, bending gently to the right as it goes.

Through a copse of ancient sugar maples, we capture a magnificent panoramic view of Lake Chautauqua. This is the grove Olmsted designated on his plan as Fountain Park. Furnished with benches arranged under the dense shade, the park is still treasured by residents as a serenely beautiful place to rest on a quiet summer afternoon. Across Lake Avenue from this park [H] is the community beach with its swimming platform and playground, a popular attraction in summer. In earlier times the point of land extending into the lake at this location served as a landing for the big lake steamers (refer back to Figure 23). It was a bustling spot in the days of the Grand Hotel and later when countless smaller hotels flourished. In summer large numbers of people, mainly from Pittsburgh and Cleveland, came to stay at the hotels and in individual residences. Often wives and children would spend the entire summer here, while husbands and fathers would travel in for the weekends. The men arrived on Friday nights at the railway station on the Mayville waterfront, took a steamer across the lake to Point Chautauqua, and returned to their city jobs on Monday.

Proceeding northward from [H] on Lake Avenue – the only extensive stretch of level road in Point Chautauqua – we follow this curving roadway along the waterfront. At Elm Park, Lake Avenue rises sharply just before it ends at

Floral. Turning right onto Floral, we continue our ascent, observing a fine, open view of the lake from this higher elevation. A few yards beyond, we enter Orchard Avenue to the right. Dipping slightly, Orchard follows an intermediate level between Floral and Lake Avenue. Orchard rounds a series of decided bends on the way to its junction with Diamond. We reenter Diamond to the right and retrace our steps back past Fountain Park to Lake Avenue [H]. This time we go to the left, following Lake Avenue southward as it winds gently along the margins of the lake.

After about a quarter of a mile, the road comes to an end before a small woodland. Here, on the left, we discover a secluded pathway leading steeply up the hill to Diamond Avenue. According to tradition, this path was not designed by Olmsted but came into being as shortcut to the lake's edge for nearby residents. Today this path is densely shaded by trees and lined with thick bushes on either side. Lemon balm grows here, and an especially lovely variety of frail wild grass. At Diamond we turn right and continue into a deep woods, site of Olmsted's Sylvan Grove, where the road ends under a street lamp that still comes on mysteriously at night, even though it is nearly overgrown by grapevines and hidden by great bushes. To the right is a vacant area overrun with wild grapevines and brush. Narcissus blooms here in the spring – also a tall variety of snowdrops, some daffodils, trout lily, and trillium. This delightful place was originally known as Olmsted's Sylvan Grove.

Retracing our steps out of the woods and back along Diamond, we turn right into Groveland, which takes us upward in a series of gradual curves past the east side of Memorial Park. Beyond its intersection with Maple, Groveland enters a thickly wooded area. The woods extend on the right of Groveland all the way to Route 430, and it occupies the space Olmsted had reserved for the Corinthian Grove and the Pavilion. It is not known how much of this area was developed in the early days; it seems fairly certain that the Pavilion was never built.

Groveland itself is one of the beauty spots of Point Chautauqua. It winds through woods on either side, with tall maples, beeches, and hickories arching high above. Groveland crosses Elm and continues as an unpaved path through another wooded area that extends behind the Tabernacle site. It ends at Leet Ave.

We now retrace the Groveland path back to Elm Avenue, which we take to the left. As we walk along Elm, we are aware that it is not an Olmsted-designed road, being perfectly straight and lacking any curvature.[35] This route was built at a later date, after the Tabernacle fell into disuse, as a shortcut between Leet and Emerald. Within the boundaries formed by Leet, Emerald, and Elm Avenues lies the triangular wooded area. Though the upper portion, where the Tabernacle used to be, has now been partially cleared for residential construction, the lower portion of the triangle remains thickly wooded. Here violets and wild strawberry cover the ground in spring, and still standing are several dead trees that are homes for jaunty pileated woodpeckers. A tiny rivulet is here – and bamboo and tiger lilies.

Beyond this triangle of woodland forming the old Tabernacle grounds, we angle to the right into Leet Avenue, where we continue to be flanked on the right by the woods until at last we reach the lower entrance to the grounds of Point Chautauqua at Highway 430 [I].

[35] Elm Avenue is one of only two Point Chautauqua roads that were not designed by Olmsted. The other is Maple Avenue.

REFERENCES

BOOKS

BARLOW, Elizabeth, and William Alex 1972. *Frederick Law Olmsted's New York*. New York: Praeger Publishers.

BEVERIDGE, Charles E., and David Schuyler 1983. *The Papers of Frederick Law Olmsted: Creating Central Park, 1857-61*. Baltimore: Johns Hopkins.

BEVERIDGE, Charles E., and Paul Rocheleau 1995. *Frederick Law Olmsted: Designing the American Landscape*. New York: Rizzoli.

BEVERIDGE, Charles E., and Paul Rocheleau 1998. *Frederick Law Olmsted: Designing the American Landscape*. (ed. by David Larkin), Rev.ed. New York: Universe Pub.

CHADWICK, George F. 1966. *The Park and the Town: Public Landscape in the Nineteenth and Twentieth Centuries*. New York: Frederick A. Praeger, Inc.

CHRISTENSEN, Carol A. 1985. *The American Garden City and the New Towns Movement* (ed. by Stephen Foster). Ann Arbor, Mich.: UMI Research Press.

CLAWSON, Marion, and Peter Hall 1973. *Planning and Urban Growth: An Anglo-American Comparison*. Baltimore: Johns Hopkins.

COMMISSION for the New Towns 1961. *Crawley New Town*. Crawley, Sussex: Hubners Ltd.

CREESE, Walter L. 1966. *The Search for Environment: The Garden City, Before and After*. New Haven: Yale University Press.

CREESE, Walter L. 1985. *Crowning of the American Landscape: Eight Great Spaces and Their Buildings*. Princeton, N.J.: Princeton University Press.

DIETER, Melvin Easterday 1980. *The Holiness Revival of the Nineteenth Century*. Metuchen, N.J.: The Scarecrow Press, Inc.

DOWNING, Andrew Jackson 1841. *A Treatise on the Theory and Practice of Landscape Gardening Adapted to North America*. New York: Wiley and Putnam.

ECCARDT, John Moss 1973. *Ebenezer Howard*. Topsfield, Mass.: Newbury Books.

ECKBO, Garrett 1946. *Urban Landscape Design*. New York: McGraw-Hill Book Company.

FABOS, J. G., G. T. Milde, and V. M. Weinmyr 1968. *Frederick Law Olmsted, Sr: Founder of Landscape Architecture in America*. Amherst: University of Mass. Press.

FEIN, Albert, ed. 1968. *Landscape Into City Scape, Frederick Law Olmsted's Plans for a Greater New York City*. Ithaca: Cornell University Press.

FEIN, Albert 1972. *Frederick Law Olmsted and the American Environmental Tradition*. New York: George Braziller.

FISHER, Irving D. 1986. *Frederick Law Olmsted and the City Planning Movement in the United States*. Ann Arbor: UMI Research Press.

FISHMAN, Robert 1977. *Urban Utopias in the 20th Century*. Cambridge, Mass.: M.I.T. Press.

GOTHEIN, Marie Luise 1966. *A History of Garden Art*, Vol. 2. New York: Hacker Art Books (first published in English in 1928).

HOWARD, Ebenezer 1946. *Garden Cities of To-Morrow.* Cambridge, Mass.: M.I.T. Press.

KAISER, Harvey H. 1978. *The Building of Cities: Development and Conflict.* Ithaca, N.Y.: Cornell University Press.

KARSON, Robin S. 1989. *Fletcher Steele, Landscape Architect: An Account of the Gardenmaker's Life.* New York: Harry N. Abrams/Sagapress, Inc.

KITCHEN, Paddy 1975. *A Most Unsettling Person: The Life and Ideas of Patrick Geddes.* London: Gollancz

KOWSKY, Francis R., ed. 1992. *Frederick Law Olmsted: Designs for Buffalo Parks and Parkways, 1868-1898.* Buffalo, N.Y.: Burchfield Art Center.

KOWSKY, Francis R., ed. 1992. *The Best Planned City: The Olmsted Legacy in Buffalo.* Buffalo, N.Y.: Burchfield Art Center.

KOWSKY, Francis R. 1998. *Country, Park & City: The Architecture and Life of Calvert Vaux.* Oxford: Oxford University Press.

LYNCH, Kevin 1960. *The Image of the City.* Cambridge, Mass.: M.I.T. Press.

LYNES, RUSSELL 1954. *The Tastemakers.* New York: Harper.

McLAUGHLIN, C. C., C. E. Beveridge, and others, eds. 1977- . *The Papers of Frederick Law Olmsted.* Baltimore: Johns Hopkins University Press.

MUMFORD, Lewis 1970. *The Culture of Cities.* New York: Harcourt, Brace.

MAIRET, Philip 1957. *Pioneer of Sociology: The Life and Letters of Patrick Geddes.* Westport, Conn.: Hyperion.

MILLER, Donald L. 1989. *Lewis Mumford: A Life.* New York: Weidenfeld & Nicolson.

NEWTON, Norman T. 1971. *Design on the Land, The Development of Landscape Architecture.* Cambridge, Mass.: Belknap Press of Harvard University Press.

OLMSTED, Frederick Law 1852. *Walks and Talks of an American Farmer in England.* London: David Bogue.

OLMSTED, Frederick Law 1856. *A Journey in the Seaboard Slave States, with Remarks on Their Economy.* New York: Dix & Edwards.

OLMSTED, Frederick Law 1860. *A Journey in the Back Country.* New York: Mason Bros.

OLMSTED, Frederick Law. *Civilizing American Cities: Writings on City Landscapes* (ed. by J. B. Sutton). New York: Da Capo Press.

OLMSTED, Frederick Law, Jr., and Theodora Kimball, eds. 1970. *Frederick Law Olmsted, Landscape Architect, 1822-1903.* New York: G. P. Putnam's Sons.

OSBORN, Frederic J. 1971. *Greenbelt Cities: The British Contribution.* London: Faber & Faber.

RASMUSSEN, Steen Eiler 1969. *Towns and Buildings.* Cambridge, Mass.: M.I.T. Press.

REPS, John W. 1965. *The Making of Urban America.* Princeton, N.J.: Princeton University Press.

132

ROBINSON, Albert J. 1975. *Economics and New Towns: A Comparative Study of the United States, the United Kingdom, and Australia.* New York: Praeger.

ROPER, Laura Wood 1973. *FLO: A Biography of Frederick Law Olmsted.* Baltimore, Md.: Johns Hopkins University Press.

RYBCZYNSKI, Witold. 1999. *A Clearing in the Distance: Frederick Law Olmsted and America in the Nineteenth Century.* New York: Scribner.

SCHUYLER, David 1986. *The New Urban Landscape: The Redefinition of City Form in Nineteenth-century America.* Baltimore: Johns Hopkins University Press.

SCHUYLER, David 1992. *The Papers of Frederick Law Olmsted: The Years of Olmsted, Vaux & Company, 1865-1874.* Baltimore: Johns Hopkins University Press.

SIMPSON, Jeffrey 1999. *Chautauqua: An American Utopia.* New York: Harry N. Abrams, Inc.

SMITH, M. H. 1963. *The History of Garden City.* Garden City, N.Y.: Garden City Press.

STAMP, L. Dudley, and Stanley H. Beaver 1958. *The British Isles: A Geographic and Economic Survey.* London: Longmans, Green and Co.

STEVENSON, Elizabeth 1977. *Park-Maker: A Life of Frederick Law Olmsted.* New York: Macmillan.

SUTTON, S. B., ed. 1971. *A Selection of Frederick Law Olmsted's Writings on City Landscapes.* Cambridge, Mass.: M.I.T. Press.

SWEET, W. W. 1944. *Revivalism in America: Its Origin, Growth and Decline.* New York: Charles Scribner's Sons.

SWEET, W. W. 1946. *Religion on the American Frontier.* Savage, Md.: Cooper Square.

SYRACUSE UNIVERSITY, 1988. *Landmarks of Oswego County.* Syracuse: Syracuse University Press.

THOMPSON, John 1970. *Geography of New York State.* Syracuse, N.Y.: Syracuse University Press.

TUNNARD, Christopher A. 1978. *A World with a View: An Inquiry into the Nature of Scenic Values.* New Haven, Conn.: Yale University Press.

TUNNARD, Christopher A., and Boris Pushkarev 1963. *Man-Made America: Chaos or Control?* New Haven, Conn.: Yale University Press.

TURNER, Roger 1985. *Capability Brown and the Eighteenth-Century English Landscape.* New York: Rizzoli International Publications, Inc.

WEISBERGER, B. A. 1958. *They Gathered at the River: The Story of the Great Revivalists and Their Impact upon Religion in America.* Boston: Little, Brown and Company.

WEISS, Ellen 1987. *City in the Woods: The Life and Design of an American Camp Meeting on Martha's Vineyard.* New York/Oxford: Oxford University Press.

WISHINSKY, Frieda 1999. *The Man Who Made Parks: The Story of Parkbuilder Frederick Law Olmsted.* Tundra Books.

WURMAN, R. S., et al. 1972. *The Nature of Recreation: A Handbook in Honor of Frederick Law Olmsted.* Cambridge, Mass.: M.I.T. Press.

WYCHERLY, R. E. 1962. *How the Greeks Built Cities*. London: Macmillan.

ZAITZEVSKY, Cynthia. 1982. *Frederick Law Olmsted and the Boston Park System*. Cambridge, Mass.: Belknap Press.

PERIODICALS

BUFFALO DAILY COURIER 1876. "Point Chautauqua," *Buffalo Daily Courier* (July 31, 1876), p. 2. [Article on Point Chautauqua, courtesy of Dr. Francis R. Kowsky].

CHAUTAUQUA ASSEMBLY HERALD 1881. "Annual Gathering of the Point Chautauqua Baptist Union" (Wed., Aug. 10, 1881).

COLE, Diane 1996. "Olmsted's Visions," *Preservation* (September/October).

HOUSE BEAUTIFUL 1989. "The Man Who Invented Landscape Architecture," *House Beautiful* (October 1989).

JAMESTOWN DAILY HERALD 1877. "Walter L. Sessions," *The Jamestown Daily Herald* (August 8, 1877). Article on the president of the Board of Management (Point Chautauqua Association).

JAMESTOWN DAILY HERALD n.d. "Point Chautauqua." [Summary of historical events at the early Point Chautauqua].

LANZ, John E. 1999. "In Early Days, Methodists Withstood Fierce Challenge from Baptists Across Lake." *The Chautauquan Daily*, Weekend Edition, August 21-22, 1999.

OLMSTED, Frederick Law 1931. "Riverside, Illinois: A Residential Neighborhood Designed Over Sixty Years Ago," selections from the papers of Olmsted & Vaux, *Landscape Architecture*, 21 (July), 256-291.

OLMSTED, Frederick Law 1952b. "The Yosemite Valley and the Mariposa Big Tree Grove," *Landscape Architecture*, 43 (October), 12-25.

WARD, Sylvanus 1876. "Point Chautauqua," *Westfield Republican* (June 4, 1876).

MAPS

FAIR POINT n.d. "Map of Fair Point" (Chautauqua Institution). [This is the map that so upset Frederick Law Olmsted because of its grid-pattern design.]

OAK BLUFFS n.d. Map of planned community of Oak Bluffs (Martha's Vineyard).

RIVERSIDE n.d. Map of Riverside, Illinois, showing its Olmsted-design roadway and park systems.

POINT CHAUTAUQUA 1880. "Map of Grounds Belonging to the Point Chautauqua Association, Meeting Place of the National Baptist Union."

TACOMA 1873. "City of Tacoma, Washington Territory." [Frederick Law Olmsted's plan for Tacoma, prepared for the Northern Pacific Railway.]

MISCELLANEOUS MATERIALS

ALLEN, Everett 1985. "Notes to Accompany Photograph Album of Point Chautauqua" (dated August 18, 1985). [Now on file with Chautauqua County Historical Society, Westfield, New York.]

AMERICAN BAPTIST HISTORICAL SOCIETY. Letter, with map, from American Baptist Historical Society, 1106 South Goodman St., Rochester, NY 14620-2532 (phone 716-473-1740), to Olaf William Shelgren, Jr.

BEVERIDGE, Charles E. 1999. "Frederick Law Olmsted." *Grove Dictionary of Art.*

BEVERIDGE, Charles E., and Carolyn F. Hoffman n.d. "Master List of Design Projects of the Olmsted Firm, 1857-1950." National Association for Olmsted Parks in conjunction with the Massachusetts Association for Olmsted Parks. [Point Chautauqua is included in this list.]

GENEVA, NEW YORK 1978. "Stick Style (1870-1880)," *Nineteenth Century Architecture in Geneva,* Geneva, New York.

LAMBERT, P., ed. 1996. *Viewing Olmsted: Photographs by Robert Burley, Lee Friedlander, and Geoffrey James.* Traveling photographic exhibit of Olmsted designs: Montreal, New York, Columbus, Ohio, Wellesley College. Montreal: Canadian Centre for Architecture.

LEET, Ernest D. 1957. "Point Chautauqua, Its Early History and Present Status of Its Roads and Highways," Jamestown, New York, May 15, 1957. [An account written by the longtime attorney for the Point Chautauqua Association and a descendent of the original homesteading family at Leet's Point (later Point Chautauqua)].

OLMSTED, Frederick Law 1875-1876. Correspondence relating to preparation of the Olmsted design for Point Chautauqua. [Photocopies of 104 pieces of correspondence are on file with the Point Chautauqua Historical Preservation Society.]

POINT CHAUTAUQUA 1975. *Point Chautauqua Centennial Issue.* Point Chautauqua, N.Y. (August 1975).

POINT CHAUTAUQUA BAPTIST UNION 1884. *Point Chautauqua Seventh Assembly, Season of 1884.* Point Chautauqua, N.Y.: Point Chautauqua Baptist Union (July 22 to August 4, 1884).

POINT CHAUTAUQUA LAND AND WATER COMPANIES 1991. Newsletter prepared by Paul H. Roese, President of the Point Chautauqua Land and Water Companies, July 1991.

TENNANT, M. D. 1875. "Point Chautauqua Notes." Undated memo to Frederick Law Olmsted (from Olmsted correspondence cited above).

N O T E S